CHANNELLING
CREATING MAGIC
FOR THE NEW AGE
BY BRAD STEIGER

WITH CONTRIBUTIONS BY
FRANCES PASCAL STEIGER

Editorial Direction & Layout:
Timothy Green Beckley

Manuscript Production:
Soltec Manuscript Service

Copyright © 1987 by Brad Steiger
All Rights Reserved

All rights reserved. No part of this book may be reproduced, stored in a retrieval system, or transmitted, in any form or by any means, electronic, mechanical, photocopying, recording, or otherwise, without prior permission of the author and publisher. Manufactured in the United States of America.

Cover and inside art as indicated is copyrighted by Annabelle Culverwell from the portfolio "IMAGO VERI" - IMAGES OF TRUTH, available from Columba Krebs, Box 529, Mt. Grove, Missouri 65711

Published by:
INNER LIGHT PUBLICATIONS
P.O. BOX 753
NEW BRUNSWICK, N.J. 08903
Current book catalog sent free upon request.

ISBN
0-938294-24-5

NEW AGE/OCCULT

CONTENTS

CHAPTER ONE:
THE POWERFUL FORCE OF MAGIC — 5

CHAPTER TWO:
THE AQUARIAN MAGICIAN MUST UNDERSTAND: THE NEW AGE HAS CHANGED THE SUN SIGNS — 13

CHAPTER THREE:
INFLUENCE OTHERS THROUGH RITUAL MAGIC — 33

CHAPTER FOUR:
DETERMINE YOUR MAGIC NUMBERS FOR SUCCESS ON YOUR LIFEPATH — 43

CHAPTER FIVE:
ALIGNING YOURSELF WITH ANGELS AND GUIDES — 53

CHAPTER SIX:
HOW TO CONTACT BENEVOLENT SPIRITS — 61

CHAPTER SEVEN:
RECEIVE AWARENESS THROUGH VISION TEACHINGS — 74

CHAPTER EIGHT:
HEALING MIRACLES CAN BE YOURS — 81

CHAPTER NINE:
THE WONDERFUL WIZARDRY OF COLORS — 93

CHAPTER TEN:
CHARMS, AMULETS AND RINGS — 100

CHAPTER ELEVEN:
CHANTS AND CEREMONIES — 109

CHAPTER TWELVE:
USING CRYSTALS FOR HIGH MAGIC — 120

Brad Steiger, author, lecturer, New Age Alchemist

CHAPTER ONE:
THE POWERFUL FORCE OF MAGIC

Genuine Magic Can Achieve All Your Desires
The Magic of ESP
Telepathy
Precognition
Mind-Over-Matter
Psychometry
Self-Healing
A Candle Meditation
Children's Natural ESP Abilities
Compel the Universe to Do Your Bidding
Ceremonial Magic
Tap the Cosmic Source

I believe in Magic.

For thousands of generations, from the earliest days of the cave dweller to Star Wars technology, Magic has served the human race. And it will be as powerful and as meaningful in the New Age.

Magic is the use of rituals, chants, ceremonies, and affirmations which are designed to give the individual control of the forces that manipulate the universe.

These forces could not care less by what names you call them. It does not matter to them if you ascribe to them the catch-phrases of contemporary science or evoke the ancient names of the Old Ones. What is important to them is that you know that the forces do exist...that they are there to be called upon and to act as powerful servants for those who have learned to control them.

And make no mistake about it. These forces can be controlled--by you! Whatever you seek in life--peace, happiness, the secret of love, the pursuit of wealth--all these things can come easily to you once you know and understand the power of True Magic.

GENUINE MAGIC CAN ACHIEVE ALL YOUR DESIRES

In the past, if a person had the power to control matter and other people, without opening his mouth and without physical implements, he would have been called a sorcerer, a magician. Today we say he has the remarkable ability of psychokinesis.

Psychokinesis, simply defined, is mind-over-mind or mind-over-matter. A person with psychokinetic abilities can will another person to act in a certain way--often contrary to his usual habits--without that other person's knowledge, and from a distance of several thousand miles. He can levitate people and objects--solely through the power of his will--and he can manifest in his life whatever things he desires, be they wealth, material possessions, or love. From all practical considerations, he is the master of his own destiny.

The name you give to the practitioner of these abilities depends upon your own spiritual orientation. If you were reared by a fundamentalist minister, you say he gets his power from the devil. If you are a devout Catholic, you say he receives his talents from God or the Holy Spirit. If you are an occultist, you say he is a white magician. If you are a scientist, you say he manifests the psi function of psychokinesis. If you lived in another era you may well have had him burned at the stake as a sorcerer and heretic.

Seen through the eyes of psychology and the parapsychic sciences, magic becomes a sound, workable system, not the bundle of superstition of which it is usually accused.

THE MAGIC OF ESP

"I don't like to call ESP a 'gift.'" David Hoy, the late master psychic once told me. "Whether in me or others it's an *ability*. Many persons use ESP in their daily affairs, but they neither recognize nor develop it."

If one would develop his extrasensory abilities Hoy believed he first must be convinced of the phenomenon's existence; then he must be persuaded to accept the possibility of his own capabilities. Acknowledgement comes first, then comes awareness. These are states of mind anyone can achieve.

For simplicity, Hoy divided ESP into three categories: *telepathy* (mind-to-mind communication), *precognition* (the ability to predict events in advance of their occurrence) and *psychokinesis* (mind-over-mind and mind-over-matter).

USING TELEPATHY TO MEET OTHERS

"Telepathy is an ability we all have which is easy to trigger," Hoy taught. "To make contact with some other person all you need do is think intently of that person and what you wish to communicate. Think of the mind as a vast reservoir of energy ready to be released into the unknown. Form the image in your mind, then let go of it and watch it float into the other person's mind."

As a gauge of your success in this exercise, Hoy suggested that you set a time limit on your thought projection, then note how long it takes to get a positive feedback or response.

You also may use telepathy to meet another person. For starters, you might try this in a room filled with people—a restaurant or some other gathering.

Pick out an individual whose back is toward you and concentrate on the back of his head.

Imagine there is a stream of light flowing from your eyes. Then on that stream send the thought, "Turn around and look at me." Don't be disappointed if your target does not turn around and look at you immediately. Just keep at it and within a few minutes he will turn, a puzzled look on his face, and stare directly at you.

Meeting someone to whom you are attracted can be accomplished in much the same manner.

"We have all been at parties where we have seen someone, of either sex, whom we would like to meet." You can arrange it telepathically, he said.

"First, concentrate on the person. Imagine the act of meeting and 'see' the introduction taking place. Send a mental photograph to that person, but don't be obvious about it. Just think on it. Soon, without your having taken a step, your `target' will come over to you and introduce himself."

None of these exercises should be forced. It is important to remain relaxed. Then when you achieve positive results, use them to cement the knowledge in your mind: *telepathy works*.

PRECOGNITION—THROWING YOUR MIND INTO THE FUTURE

The second category of psychic ability is precognition. A successful prognosticator can see into his friends' future and into his own, and he will know in advance what will take place on the international scene.

To develop this ability, you must use what Hoy terms "time-projected empathy." This is "throwing" one's mind into the future, waiting for an image to come into focus, seeing it happen, then verbalizing it. In this way you may "empathize" with the future.

"You will have misses at first," David warned, "but don't let that discourage you. It is unimportant whether you are right when you begin. What is important is that you *feel* an event as if it were actually happening in your mind."

To judge your success, however, Dave insisted on three criteria:

First you must relate your prediction to friends well in advance of the event. They then can provide substantiation.

Second, you should set a time limit in which the foreseen event must occur. (You can train yourself to do this by demanding that a time approximation accompany each impression of the future.

Third, you must record your predictions in writing in order to keep a running score.

Perhaps most important in training precognitive abilities is to *trust the images you receive*. Don't worry about the misses.

The final category of ESP is psychokinesis or PK, mind-over-mind and mind-over-matter.

MIND OVER MATTER

"Many expert gamblers believe they can control the fall of the dice and equally skilled poker players insist they can influence the cards dealt to them," Hoy stated emphatically. "Try it," he urged. "There is probably a deck of cards in your house right now, lying face down in some drawer. Select the card you think is third from the top and check to see if you are right."

This exercise is easily practiced. While shuffling the deck of cards, simply *will* a particular card to be third or fifth or seventh card from the top.

Moving from control of inanimate objects to the human mind poses ethical problems. Is controlling another's mind dangerous?

David admitted that it may hold certain risks, but he maintained that it is "not any more dangerous than other aspects of science which man either can use or abuse."

To facilitate development of this ability, Hoy suggested the following exercise:

"The next time you are out with friends for the evening, choose a course of action for one of them to follow that will manifest in some frustration. Obliquely, send out an image of your friend doing something unusual--putting the wrong end of a cigarette in his mouth, for example, or tripping up a stairway. By choosing something he normally would not do, you will know that you have been successful when he does it."

Many other facets of extrasensory perception will aid in your unfoldment. Hoy's big three--telepathy, precognition and psychokinesis--have many subdivisions and minor offshoots. Indeed, each phase of extrasensory ability is part of a vast system of tributaries. Eventually all these tributaries flow into the same great river, your own reservoir of extrasensory perception.

PSYCHOMETRY

Psychometry is one of these tributaries. To psychometrize, one holds an object belonging to another person and from that object picks up impressions of its owner. As in all aspects of ESP you must believe that the phenomenon exists and that you personally are capable of doing it.

Practice psychometry by holding an object belonging to someone you do not know well. (It proves nothing if you divulge information about a very good friend.) The most important thing to remember is to verbalize your impressions. Don't be afraid that you are wrong. Have the courage to say what you feel.

SELF-HEALING

Even self-healing may be possible through ESP. Naturally, serious medical problems require competent medical treatment--but what about the minor complaints that daily beset us all? Who does not have a common cold, usually several times a year? And who does not suffer with that painful result of high-pressure living, the tension headache? Well, David Hoy, for one.

"I haven't had a cold for at least five years," Hoy declared in lecture halls around the country. "Every time I feel the sniffles coming on I say, 'I do not want to have a cold.' This simple process is amazingly effective.

"Every day your body produces chemical substances which keep you alive. Through psychokinesis you can activate the manufacture of these chemicals with your mind.

"For example, the next time you feel a headache coming on, say to yourself, 'I call upon all my bodily resources to cure this headache. My body now will produce whatever is needed to cure this headache.' Try it. See if through psychokinesis you can control your own body."

The concentration necessary for these extrasensory abilities to manifest can be achieved more easily by some persons through the art of meditation. Hoy advocated for beginners a simple but effective means of meditating which does not involve long hours of silence or any special expertise. It is a direct method that uses the time-honored tool of the occult--the candle.

A CANDLE MEDITATION

Hoy instructed his students to place a lighted candle on a bare table, the flame 30 inches from the forehead. While the color of the candle is not important, purple traditionally is believed to be most conducive to the manifestation of ESP.

Now it is advisable to blink several times, for you shortly will begin to stare at the flame for a certain length of time without blinking.

"The pineal gland is located in the center of the brain. This is known as the 'third eye.' It is this gland that you will activate in this exercise," Hoy explained.

"Now stare intently at the flame of the candle. Examine it carefully without blinking. See that there are many colors in the flame of a candle, colors you have not noticed before.

"Watch the flame burn. Let the image of the flare sear your third eye. After 30 to 60 seconds, let your eyes slowly close, then turn upward and inward, concentrating on the center of the brain, the home of the third eye. If you have meditated properly, suddenly in all its glory the flame of the candle will appear in the middle of your forehead. As you hold the image on the screen of your mind, it will appear that it is burning its way into you. It will be a most pleasant experience. Relax and slowly open your eyes.

"As you rest in this relaxed state you may find that your mind is filled with telepathic images. Sort these out and determine with whom you have been in contact."

No words on the development of ESP would be complete without attention to the natural psychic abilities of children. In the formative years between birth and the age of five, extrasensory perception most often manifests.

CHILDREN'S NATURAL ESP ABILITIES

"Until a child reaches that point in his life when inhibitions push down his natural creative capacity, his creativity expresses itself in every form of ESP we know," David Hoy learned. "With the advent of sophisticated speech, however, the child finds that he no longer needs to rely on ESP. He then loses it, but only because he doesn't use it. For the rest of his life it will lie dormant, a vast resource of the mind just waiting to be tapped."

Because this natural ability in children is suppressed, an untold number of natural psychics are lost to the world. This conviction contributed to David Hoy's fervor for helping youth and adults regain the powers of that lost world.

"ESP is a natural facet of the human mind," he said matter-of-factly. "It is an ability anyone can develop to a high degree of proficiency."

COMPEL THE UNIVERSE TO DO YOUR BIDDING

One of the earliest of magical concepts was that the part contained the whole, and if the part could be controlled, so could the whole.

Paleolithic hunters believed that owning some fur or a bone from a stag enhanced their luck in hunting stags. By acting out the hunt and slaughter of the beast prior to the actual hunt, and by the complete subjectiveness of this experience, primitive man believed that the objective experience would also be his.

Our predecessors used this magic to gain certain ends, to fulfill desires. They believed that if they could only learn the right approach, the universe could be compelled to do man's bidding. Beliefs such as this arose because early man ascribed a consciousness, or a "spirit," to every inanimate object. Just as one can obtain a favor from another person if that person is persuaded properly, so could one similarly obtain favors from these spirits.

Certain things were thought to be the province of different spirits, factors--such as control of weather, knowledge of the future, fertility--that were beyond the control of man. If one could not control the phenomenon, then one could at least try to influence the decision-maker behind that phenomenon.

TAP THE COSMIC SOURCE

Magic can be woven into the fabric of contemporary living, no matter how complex a schedule you have. Moments can be culled from the day's work and assembled before bedtime for ritual work.

For the more complex ceremonies a greater amount of time is needed, but for certain elementary rituals 15 minutes to a half hour are all that is needed. Absolute quiet is preferable, but you can learn to blot out extraneous sounds and perform your rituals regardless.

Keep a record of what works, what does not work, what factors you think contributed to the success of a particular ritual. Do not become manipulators of coincidence, gullible enough to believe you have actually effected something without having first verified it.

Magic is the use of rituals designed to give the individual--you--control of the forces that manipulate the universe. Magic can be and has been used for centuries to obtain for its practitioners love, wealth, material possessions, good health, long life. These things are also available to you, as they are available to anyone who learns to tap the cosmic source.

Frances Pascal Steiger explains an intricate metaphysical concept to Brad and to the audience at a seminar.

CHAPTER TWO:
THE AQUARIAN MAGICIAN MUST UNDERSTAND: THE NEW AGE HAS CHANGED THE SUN SIGNS

Signs in the Heavens
The Stars Speak
Legacy of the Star Beings
The Tenth Planet
The Cosmic Cycle
The Divine Plan
The Grand Cosmic Cycle
The Age of Polarity
The Death Throes of Pisces
The Great Division
The Coming Age of Harmony
A Quantum Leap for Earth
The End-Times
An Age of Unity
A New Religion
The New Man
Our Solar Initiation
Your Astrological Sun Sign in the New Age

SIGNS IN THE HEAVENS

THE Bible contains many references to the division of time, of Ages long since past. Of the Age of Pisces, the fish; of Aries, the ram; of Taurus, the cow or bull. It tells also of the signs and the wonders that will appear in the heavens during the last days of the Age of Pisces:

"And it shall come to pass in the last days," saith God, "I will pour out my Spirit on all flesh; and your sons and your daughters shall prophesy, and your young shall see visions; and your old shall dream dreams. And I shall show wonders in Heaven above and signs in the Earth below..."
Acts 2:17-19

The sun, the moon, and particularly those planets that occupy our solar system are believed to affect all that is on Earth, for electromagnetic energies emanate from planetary bodies. Since the entire universe is composed of E-M particles, all is affected. With matter, there is time; and in this realm of space and time there is a birth and a death on a physical level of all matter, of all energy, as they transit through various stages.

Police departments, psychologists, and caretakers of mental institutions have noted that during certain phases of a moon's cycle the minds of people are definitely affected to greater or lesser degrees, dependent on the individual psyche's balance. All agree that it is the full moon that adversely affects those people with a weak or imbalanced mind. More ravings, more madness, and more crime occur during a full-moon's cycle than at any other time of the month.

Some theorize that since the moon affects the oceans, causing the tides to rise and fall, and because the human body is largely water, the magnetic pull of a full moon on the chemicals of the mind imbalances a weak-willed person. How this works no one knows, only that it does. The phenomenon has been noted for thousands of years, hence the word "lunatic," from *luna* meaning moon madness, as well as the well-known legend of the wolf-man, whose madness overtook him during the full moon.

THE STARS SPEAK

The stars "speak" through the Sun's entry into the Zodiac, the circle of the animal patterns that twinkle in the night sky.

Some people believe the ancient art of astrology, the ability to interpret what the stars are saying, and that of astronomy, the science of the stars, came from the Chaldeans, the Babylonians, the Sumerians. Others suggest that the Atlanteans, fleeing their doomed land, brought this knowledge with them to those countries to which they fled. There are those who believe this ancient means of divination was given to Earth's people from beings who descended to Earth from the stars.

LEGACY OF THE STAR-BEINGS

The beliefs of the Sumerians and the beings from the stars were one to the ancient people who occupied the region in the lower Euphrates River valley. The Sumerians wrote on stone tablets about "gods" who descended from a star, walked across the river waters, and taught the people all that they would come to know. The Star-gods gave them the science of astronomy, as well as astrology, and taught them techniques of medicine, agriculture, and architecture.

The Star-beings also gave them the means of recording all these things through the cuneiform language, the first written word. Our contemporary arts and sciences are all based on the primary discoveries of these ancient people.

Science chooses not to believe what the Sumerians say occurred, but the facts remain. *Something* happened, for these simple people made a quantum leap in their cultural advancement and established a society so wondrous as to defy orthodox, scientific explanation.

On a Sumerian cylinder seal that dates back to 2,500 B.C. there exists the pictorial representation of our solar system. There is clearly shown a Star-sun in the center with ten (10) planets revolving around it.

It wasn't until the 16th century that Copernicus would shock the academicians of his time, as well as the all-powerful churchstate link-up, with his findings that the sun was in the center of our solar system and the planets evolved around it. Since this discovery went against the church's understanding of the universe, people were imprisoned and persecuted for teaching Copernicus' new science. Anyone could clearly see that the Earth was the center of the universe. Didn't the sun rise in the east and set in the west?

It was not until the 18th century that scientific astronomers sighted Uranus. Neptune was finally discovered in the 19th century. Pluto was found in our own century.

We have only nine planets in our solar system; however, and we are still one short of the ten planets depicted by the ancient Sumerians.

THE TENTH PLANET

It will not be until the end of the 20th century that we will discover that other planet. By all indications, according to our finest observatories and our most sophisticated equipment, another planet exists beyond the ninth planet, Pluto. In fact, it is guessed to be quite possibly as large as the planet Jupiter, because of certain gravitational calculations.

Now that would finally bring us up to the ten planets noted by the ancient Sumerians, who said they were given such futuristic knowledge by people that descended from the stars.

THE COSMIC CYCLE

Basically, the dates of the Sun's entry into each successive Zodiacal sign varies somewhat from year to year due to time passing through what is known as a Cosmic Cycle composed of 25,920 years. But the approximate dates for one's own Sun Sign are: Aries, March 21; Taurus, April 20; Gemini, May 20th; Cancer, June 21; Leo, July 22; Virgo, August 23; Libra, September 23; Scorpio, October

23; Sagittarius, November 22; Capricorn, December 21; Aquarius, January 20; and Pisces, February 19.

The first sign of the zodiac is *Aries*, the Ram. Briefly, Aries is known for its pioneering instinct, its initiative, its leadership.

Taurus has courage, endurance, and loyalty to whatever it deems to be important.

Gemini is recognized for its versatility, its vitality, its energy.

Cancer is known for attunement, sympathy and empathy.

Leo is cited for its ability to love with great strength, its affinity for authority, and its integrity.

Virgo is recognized for its industry, its attention to detail, its simplistic attitude toward complex matters.

Libra is noted for harmony, fairness, and balance --the justice of weighing all things.

Scorpio has the ability to conform with keen survival instincts, and control over life's situations.

Capricorn is recognized for its tenacious spirit, its ability to cling to traditional values, its depth in regard to the importance of physical earth.

Aquarius is noted for its humaneness, its equalitarian attitude, its fellowship, its tendency toward inventiveness and its genius..

Pisces has spiritual qualities which deal with the physical, the dualism of the psyche, the division of all things for a greater purpose.

THE DIVINE PLAN AND THE AGE OF AQUARIUS

I have received through my channeling that the Zodiac is like a massive clock whose complex machinations, its interworkings, were created to act as a guiding influence of the Divine Plan.

In the beginning the Source devised a Plan that would permit it to grow, to expand, to increase in complexity and thereby to experience life in a myriad of forms and dimensions. The Source caused countless energies to exist on many levels of reality and these energy systems created other forms of energy which were patterned after their interaction with other forms of matter.

Since each energy system is electromagnetic, it gathers the energies of "fruits" that it created from its particular experiences, thereby increasing and elevating its own vibrations--and thus evolving ever upward in its eventual return to the Source. As energy returns to its Source and brings with it all that it created and gathered to it, it permits the Source to expand, to increase in complexity and to experience life in a multitude of forms and dimensions. All will be for the glory of God and the benefit of all who join with It.

The monthly zodiac and its influence on all matter goes forward, just as time marches onward, as a clock goes forward in its motion recording the passing of time. But being electromagnetic, there is a polarity to all things of matter.

Zodiacal Ages, twelve in a Cosmic Cycle, operate in reverse, just as electro-magnetic properties operate in a reverse, or counter-clockwise, motion; just as the E-M energies of Earth cause it to spin counterclockwise. We are now about to leave the Age of Pisces, of division, and enter the next astrological sign, the Age of Aquarius, that of harmony. Yes, it is the dawning of the Age of Aquarius that we will begin experiencing quite strongly in the mid-90's.

THE GRAND COSMIC CYCLE

Eacn age of a Grand Cosmic Cycle lasts 2,160 years. And with 12 zodiacal signs being a part of it, a Grand Cycle lasts 23,920 years. *All* that exists in the realm of matter is affected by the E-M vibrations of whatever Age is in reign, no matter what monthly astrological sign denoted its birth.

Each age has a life of its own. It has a birth, builds to a peak, slowly "ages," and then passes on as if dying. The writings, legends, and lore of Earth's ancient people indicate that Ages frequently pass on or go out with a bang.

Because the Age of Pisces was one of division, it is more than likely that great divisions will continue to take place in all aspects of life--that of the spirit (churchly matters)...of the mind...the division of positive and negative...of feminine and masculine...of the right-half and the left-half of the brain. All of matter being physical naturally and artificially created, such as corporations, and institutions. The Earth, being of matter, should also divide, there being great changes in the seasons and the land masses dividing, with great floodings.

Since an Age, being 2,160 years, is electromagnetically governed, it affects all of matter with its birth, its life, and its death. An Age is affected by time, just as we are affected by it. In our infancy we do not have our greatest strength, but gradually gain it as we continue to mature. So does an Age gain in strength, reaching its peak in mid-life. It then continues on, slowly aging until it dies, just as we pass away.

The mid-time of an Age is 1,080 years, give or take several hundred years. This is when its greatest strengths are evident, when it expresses the qualities it was created for.

As it nears its end, an Age may rally forth, showing some of its earlier strengths, its natural characteristics --just as a person before dying is seen to gain strength and rally for a time before passing on. The death of an Age occurs so that another might be born, so that the Divine Plan of evolution--that of energy and matter--might be fulfilled, for such was the purpose of all creation.

Let's look at the peak of the Piscean Age of polarity, of division: 2,160 divided in half equals 1,080. Since the Age of Pisces began in -60 B.C. that would make the years 1020 to 1300 A.D. the peak time of Pisces, when its greatest strengths would be felt.

In the year 1021 A.D., Caliph al-Hakim proclaimed himself divine and founded the Druse sect, gaining many followers. The Druse are a sect of people whose creed was derived from Moslem, Christian, and Persian sources.

In the year 1095 A.D., the First Crusade was launched to free the Holy Places from the Saracens (Muslims). Individual Crusaders would begin the journey in August 1096. The victories of the First Crusade were in large part due to the Crusaders' not confronting a *united* Muslim world, but rather, with a number of isolated divisions of a weakened Muslim power. Thus Jerusalem was captured by the crusading Christians on orders of the Holy Church of Rome.

In 1208 Pope Innocent III proclaimed a Crusade against the Albigenses, a religious sect in southern France. Crusaders came from all provinces located to the north, for they were envious of the Albigenses' great culture and wealth. This was the only crusade to be ordered against fellow Christians, and over a million people were slain who were followers of the Holy Ghost, rather than the Holy Church of Rome.

In 1291 the Saracens (Muslims) captured Acre, last Christian stronghold in Palestine. This was the end of the Crusades.

Since Pisces represents both the spirit and the flesh in division, two fish swimming in opposite directions, the all-powerful rulers, who had blended Church and State, declared war and death to all people who threatened its sovereignty.

THE DEATH THROES OF PISCES

We are now in the death throes of the Piscean Age. It is rallying forth with as much strength as it can muster before it passes on.

Looking through a glass darkly, we can see the faint glimmer of what occurred at Pisces' peak, its mid-time, the Crusades. Now once again in a smaller way, as a more weakened Pisces begins to pass, great divisions will occur, together with the threat of once again combining church and state for total power and control.

Surely in the last hundred years we have seen the glimmer of great division and the ensuing struggle to the death that has and will occur. Two World Wars have occurred during the 20th century with many minor wars continuing to occur. Persecution because of one's belief construct brought the Holocaust and the death of millions of innocent people. The invention and the use of the splitting of an atom precipitated the bombing of two cities in Japan by the United States.

THE GREAT DIVISION

We have suffered the division and the religious war of Ireland, which still burns on; the division and the persecutions suffered by Ghandi and his people; the division and religious persecution of the Sikhs for the mistreatments they felt were dealt them by the reigning power of Indira Ghandi, who, like the Ghandi before her, was assassinated.

Then there is the division that is coming again to the Church of Rome, as it argues with the feminine principle, the power of the first principle of the Trinity. Catholic women are demanding equal service to God, a fair share of power and purpose.

There will be a great division seen in all churches, for there will be those who will agree that God is male to the exclusion of the feminine principle; and there will be those who believe God is both male and female, both the creative and the guiding principles --the feminine principle creating and the masculine principle guiding the energies thus created. The churches will be divided, and those that do not unite harmoniously on the balance of it will continue to divide amongst themselves until finally they cease to exist, being of the past and not involved with the evolution of its own energy.

The U.S. Geological Survey says that the many faults that line the coasts of America, particularly that of California, are overdue for their division. Great land masses, earthquakes, tidal waves, floodings, and dramatic changes in weather and vulcanism is beginning to occur.

Still remember, each coming New Age has its heralders, its soothsayers, its wisepeople, its leaders, to help in its purpose of the Plan of all life on Earth.

As the Age of Pisces passes from us, we have the greatest possibility of unity. Yes, we have a choice. We can swim in opposing directions or unite for peace and harmony.

THE COMING AGE OF HARMONY

The coming Age of Aquarius is the most harmonious of all Ages. Violet is the color of the Age of Aquarius, and the psyche, the mind of all living things, its energies on every level of existence will be affected by the violet of the coming New Age.

According to NASA, the Jupiter Effect, the solar system's planets coming into their alignment, will cause an increase of solar activity, as much as 20 per cent, which will result in many sun storms, thereby giving forth intensified ultra-violet radiation, showering it on Earth. Also, scientists say that the ozone layer, which protects Earth from ultra-violet radiations, is slowly being eaten away by the pollutions that are dumped into our atmosphere by the billions of tons daily.

When infra-red is applied in a small measure to the psyche of people there is seen a quicker reflex of hand-to-eye movement. Ultra-violet, applied in small measure to the human psyche or animal psyche, will increase the functioning of the brain, the subconscious and the conscious, right and left half, and their interworkings.

Those parts of our brain not being used (science estimates this is 80 to 90 percent) will begin in their functioning. The Earth's magnetic field will be affected by the bioelectric field, as will the nervous system of all living things, as will all matter.

A QUANTUM LEAP FOR EARTH

Earth will experience a quantum leap never before witnessed, as it lunges toward its Source, its Creator --as it rushes in its performance of the Divine Plan of harmonious energies being created and evolutionized on a migration to the Source of all things. No longer will Earth's people be mired in earthly matters, but they will have a cosmic, spiritual perspective, that of a universal consciousness.

AN AGE OF UNITY

Those living during the Age of Aquarius, with its birth throes coming during the 1990's, will--and must --become accustomed to change; for many changes will occur, and they will come quickly. Those who can't adjust to change will choose division, and their interworkings will divide against themselves, their mind, their system. Their bodies will thus deteriorate in their functioning, for the Age of Division is dying, and the Age of Unity of Equality is being born.

Aquarius, symbolized by a waterboy bearing a pitcher of water, will see a transformation of its sign to that of a watergirl, or waterwoman; for Aquarius will bring in the feminine vibration, in equal strength with the masculine vibration. With her pitcher filled with spiritual energy, she will pour forth the Holy Spirit on the world, affecting the minds of all people, all living things. Both the conscious and the subconscious mind will come into balance. A holism will exist in all things.

The feminine aspect of the Creator, the creative aspect of God, will be recognized, rather than just the guiding, masculine aspect.

As reflections of the Source, the feminine creative aspect of our subconscious mind will be made strong in its dominion; and the masculine guiding aspect of our conscious mind will direct its creations into being. Think of these things when you consider your Sun Sign.

A NEW RELIGION

A new religion will surface over the Earth. Those churches that continue to exist will be transformed in their workings, adjusting to the New Age. They will serve as gathering places, helping those assembled to self-evolve, rather than be controlled.

There will be a balancing in church leaders, for women as well as men, girls as well as boys, will serve forth their energies equally to the people.

All that is optimistic, idealistic, and harmonious will be expressed by the existing religions, rather than pessimistic, divisionistic, or destructive teachings. Heaven will be stressed rather than hell; God, rather than satan; unity rather than division; equality, rather than the "chosen" and those cast aside. Thereby a "New Jerusalem" will surely be seen on Earth. A new Earth will be born, one in which all will rejoice.

No one will violate another's way, but aid them if need be. The ego of each individual will be sublimated with the concern for the All. Selflessness will prevail --not to the imbalance of self, but to the balance of all things.
Love will be given unconditionally to all living things. People will not exploit one another, nor will they exploit other living things. Nothing will be destroyed for the pleasure of another.
Earth will no longer be debased, but will be respected and revered. All that lives will also be treated thusly.

THE NEW MAN

Mankind will no longer desecrate or exploit the life-force. No longer will men kill for boundaries, territories, property, wealth, power. No longer will men exploit the lives of humans, animals, and other life forms for their own self-aggrandizement, for own gratification. A new male will be born, one that is balanced and harmonious to other energies, not given to destruction. Many of these New Age males are now surfacing all over planet Earth.//
With such a transformation occurring on the planet, racial prejudice, sexual prejudice, animal prejudice --all that comes forth from the ego--will pass from us.
One principal sin or trespass will be recognized and that is the violation of the energy from its evolution toward its return to the Source from which it came. We are not to violate the energy of others nor to hinder their way of going, for in doing so we also violate our own energy. We violate the Divine Plan. We violate God, Source of all there is.
Science and religion will be seen as One. No longer will they be in conflict.
Through an in-depth study of electromagnetic vibrations and with the creation of certain E-M measuring instruments, it will become obvious that an original Source--an Energy capable of designing ways to perpetuate itself, to increase its energy-needs--created all of life. This will be realized in the noted inter-workings of all matter, particularly that of living matter.
Science will thereby prove God did exist; and furthermore, it will be realized that in order to accomplish

the plan designed, the original energy quite probably *still* exists.

THE END-TIMES

During the end-times of the Age of Pisces, there will be an overwhelming need for some people to cling to yesteryear, just as we now see evident in our trends, our fashions, our return to the simplicity of the country--with country music, country movies, country clothings. Many people appear to need the security of Earth with the advent of space travel technology.

Others will grab for the future, for the Age of Aquarius, for equality, for those of like-minds, so that their force be strengthened from the E-M energies of one another, so that their goals be realized.

The black and white reality of the Piscean Age will fade into a balanced grey. It will be a time of sisterhood and brotherhood, of humanhood where humaneness prevails. All people will respond with kindness, tenderness, and mercy.

All races will be equal and will be equally treated. All sexual preferences will be recognized as to their own contribution--be they feminine, masculine, homosexual, bisexual, androgynous or asexual. There will be but one human race on Earth, and all will work together to eliminate world hunger, world suffering, world pain. Truly, it will be a Golden Age that will surpass all that have preceded it.

As a caterpillar emerges from its chrysalis to become a beautiful butterfly, so will Earth; and each Sun Sign will emerge from its division to attain great gainings, which were withheld throughout ages past.

The New Age Person, no matter what his or her sign, will break from confinements into what humans should now be. All transformed will thus be Christened by the spiritual energies of the Holy Spirit that will pour forth on the Earth, and the gifts of the spirit will be given to all.

People will be as if with one mind when it comes to all of humanity. Telepathy will be commonplace. The probabilities of one's destiny will be better controlled, thus we will create our own future with greater realization of what we truly wish.

We will operate on a creative level. We will no longer be destructive, and we will have unconditional love for one and all living things.

THE RETURN OF MOTHER ISIS

The energies of the ruling planet of Aquarius, Uranus, the seventh planet, which means "heaven," will be boosted by a tenth planet soon to be discovered in our solar system at the end of the 20th century.

An apt name for the tenth planet might be Isis, for surely its energy is that of the feminine creative principle, a Mother's vibration. Isis, you might recall, was believed by the Egyptians to be the being who civilized them and who was bearer of the creative energy of the Sun, which she wore on her head like a halo, sometimes wearing the horns of a cow, symbolic of her mothering principle.

With the spiritual energies of the mother-creator being recognized and shown on horoscope charts, a greater awareness and a clearer understanding of one's life and the universal consciousness of the New Age will be obtained. Our planetary solar system will at last reflect the astrological awareness given the Sumarians many thousands of years ago when they depicted the star-sun and 10 planets evolving around it. And as their civilization was enlightened and their culture made a quantum-leap, ours, too, will see a similar transformation in the dawning of the Age of Aquarius.

YOUR SOLAR INITIATION

As the Age of Aquarius will increasingly be experiencing its birth throes, which will reach their height in the mid-90's, as the Age of Pisces passes on, we will begin to receive our solar initiation into the New Age, as unity and oneness begins to reign over Earth. All who are ready will receive it. Others will have their last chance to make the proper decision and to swim in the direction of the "right" fish--toward spirituality and universal consciousness. The Age of Division is leaving, and an Age of Spirituality is coming forth to reign.

With this understanding of what will come and a knowledge of your own sign's traits, you will more fully understand just how you personally will be affected. You are in a unique position, that of seeing one age die and another begin.

And how remarkable it is, for a greater extreme from Age to Age has never been seen before by humankind. Not only are we going from "division" to "oneness," but we are evolutionizing closer to our Source of origin. We will have the opportunity to achieve a greater oneness with the God energy and to experience true harmony.

GEMINI: You will get your way as never before, for your attractive, active, energetic personality will bring you great respect. You will charm the bark off of every tree in your path. All you meet upon whom you center your energies will respond to the energies you radiate. Dependent on your awareness, those people with whom you decide to interrelate will grant you all that you desire.

You will gain greater self-control and learn to crystalize your energies so that you might attain the goals which before seemed just beyond your reach. Your affectionate, generous nature will be tempered by those acts that will better aid those around you in regard to the bigger picture. You will give others gifts of the spirit and the mind, rather than the body.

Your impulsive behavior and your quick temper will become mellowed, and you will no longer have to be bewildered or hurt by the reactions you generate in others. Your high mind and your powers of observation will be enhanced in the New Age.

You will be more realistic in all that you choose to do. Thereby, your moodiness will be dissipated, for it sprang from dealing more from the body and the mind and not enough from the spirit. To your goals!

CANCER: Your energies will reach places of which you've only dreamt. The feminine energies of the Age of Aquarius will enhance your mothering nature, causing you to widen your areas of activity as never before. Those to whom you minister your energies will feel they have received a blessing.

Your straightforward, generous manner and your loyalty will be more greatly appreciated; and you will be given far more important commissions, assignments and duties to tend. Whereas previously your attention was more devoted to your foundation, in the New Age you will be more concerned with the future, which will give you even greater balance than your sign is noted for.

Your powers of concentration and your perceptiveness will know no bounds, and you will improve the lives of all those who seek you out. You will more easily express yourself, and your energies will no longer be sporadic. You will gain much foreknowledge of coming events and be able to prepare a better reaction to them. With patience and fortitude, you will accomplish things others only dream of attaining. To your future!

Generally speaking, here are some of the ways your astrological sun sign will be affected in the dawning of the Age of Aquarius. Listed are various ways your life will be transformed.

YOUR ASTROLOGICAL SUN SIGN IN THE NEW AGE

ARIES: Your ability to lead and your fondness of leadership will be aimed toward guiding others who need your assistance into discovering ways to enhance their lives. Dependent on your own awareness, you will aid others to deal better with life's problems. You will stress that they simplify and better organize their life.

Your daring, courageous nature will be stretched to the heights of your awareness, and your energetic ways will lead you into areas you never before dared to venture. Meditate on those areas that will bring you the greatest changes before making your decision. Be certain you have made the correct choice, then act accordingly.

Your aggressive determination will aid you to forge ahead into those areas of the mind where you've never before ventured. You will aid your own awareness, and you will become a greater leader in whatever field you choose. Lead on, Aries!

TAURUS: Your magnetic nature and tenacious spirit will permit you to attract those things to you that will lend to your energy, enriching your domain. The boundaries of your territory will be greatly increased, and you will apply, with firm determination, the strength of your convictions on those whose lives you touch.

You can be somewhat impersonal, but your sensitivity will extend itself beyond those with whom you are personally involved. Thereby, dependent on your awareness, you will conquer those obstacles placed in your path as never before, and you will emerge the victor.

Your easy-going nature will be better balanced in that you will declare the boundaries of what others should expect from you in advance. You will not be placed in a position to take and take until you explode, as often happened to you in the past.

All that you select to be a part of your reality will be better chosen in that you will be permitted to blossom forth and to expand to your total potential. No longer will your choices be restrictive. To your wise choice!

LEO: Known for your sympathetic heart and your physical constitution, your powers of heart and body will be boosted by the Age of Aquarius now dawning. You will, with greater balance of spirit, bring others to your depth of understanding and accomplish much for the rights of others, helping in the transformation.

As an orator, your energy will assist others to become more aware. Your idealism will be tempered, preventing you from being so easily hurt. Those Leos having no pride or false pride will have the opportunity to develop true self-esteem.

In the New Age, the leadership abilities of the Leo will be brought into sharper focus. Dependent on your awareness, you will have greater control of yourself, your attitudes, your generosities, your anger, and your forceful ways. What will emerge will be a dynamic, forceful individual who will have considerable ability to influence others, thereby accomplishing your goals.

Your ability to have your own way of thinking (with the exception of love and romantic affairs) will be greatly enhanced, for you will gain a more holistic perspective, which will aid you in your lovelife as well.

You have fought with the need to be perfect. Some of you Leos have given up altogether. In the New Age, such an achievement will be within your grasp. To your accomplishments!

VIRGO: Under the sign of the harvester, you will finally reap what you sow, for you are a giver of your energies. Dependent on your awareness in the dawning of the New Age, you will receive your due reward, thus much will return to you more immediately upon your giving.

Having a basic, natural aptitude for learning, the powers of your mind will make a quantum leap. Your attention to detail and your powers of observation will be put to greater use than ever before.

Being a natural politician, your demeanor will command the respect it deserves; for you are sensitive and diplomatic and deserving of great admiration.

You will learn to criticize the failings of others in a more constructive manner, for you will become better at understanding their ways. In a detached way, you will accomplish far more than you ever thought possible. Your honesty, sincerity, and trustworthiness, already commendable, will be realized, thus you will be better understood.

Curbing your impulsiveness and exercising self-control will be within your reach, for with the coming feminine principle, which governs the subconscious mind, your intuitive powers will be enhanced; and you will gain a deeper understanding of all that you meticulously observe.

Your fears will become "grounded," for you will have a greater awareness of coming dangers. Your new insights may prevent these hazards from happening, which will be far better than permitting fears to carry you away. Holism brings greater balance. To your harvest!

LIBRA: Your ability to externalize all that you intuitively know will be brought to the fore, thereby permitting many others to benefit from your awareness. Your attitude toward fairness will be enhanced by an even greater balancer, that of the New Age, as the powers of your subconscious mind aid your ability to see the total picture. You will perceive a holistic viewpoint; and with the great power of your mind, particularly your quickwittedness, you will instantly judge the value, strength, and worth of a matter, causing you to react better to all events and situations.

The sharpness of your tongue will be softened, for your kind and sympathetic nature never wished to wound or offend, but the quickness of your mind replied from a personal position which will now have a wider horizon. Your love of beauty and symmetry will be appreciated by those of the Age of Aquarius, for harmony and balance will reign supreme. Chaos and discord will be shunned in all forms. Your natural talents in the creative arts will be gratefully received, and all that you create--be it art, music or dance--will be welcomed.

Your extreme sensitivity, your emotional responses, will come into greater balance, for others will be more aware and will not wish to hurt you and you will thereby be able to drop your guard. In your dislike for injustice, you will understand that your extreme sensitivity has sometimes caused you to act unjustly.

But this awareness will come after you gain a different and better-for-you type of detachment, that of universal consciousness, rather than wearing a shell or withdrawing.

Using the great powers of your creative imagination to discover the ways to realize your goals will come easy to you. You will no longer feel trapped, wondering just how to accomplish what you desire, for accomplish it you will. The tender love you feel will be more fully expressed in this New Age of Unconditional Love. To your creativity!

SCORPIO: As a representative of the procreative system of humanity, the abundance of your electromagnetic energy, coming from your first chakra, your generative organs, will boost your spiritual energies as well as those of your heart. Thus your relationships with others will take on more holistic proportions in that your center will be expanded. As your spiritual self emerges, you will be the victor over the material world. Your active mind, your positive will, and your keen perception will be put to greater use, aiding all of humanity.

Because of your transformation, you will cease to be capable of such great fury and anger in your dealings with others, particularly when they do not live up to your high expectations.

The intense energy of your body will cause many of you Scorpios to elevate the energies of those people existing in your ever-widening circle and to help them to attain greater balance on every level of their being. As meticulous observers with a natural tendency to pay close attention to detail, you will serve others well, helping them to react better to those situations to which they may be slow to respond.

Your ability to think and to act to emergency situations will be used to aid others, as well as yourself; thus you will be an even more effective manager of people. Your outspokenness, your aggressive behavior, and your extreme passion, will be mellowed, and the energy will be put to greater use. This permits your great affection to be better expressed, reaching greater numbers of people. To your total emergence!

SAGITTARIUS: Your honesty, sincerity, and trustworthiness will serve you well in the now dawning Age of Aquarius. Your charitable ways, your sensitivity, will be put to great use during the coming time of change, as the Age of Pisces fades away and a New Age begins.

Your ability to draw people to you and command their respect will not be misused, for it is not natural to you to act in an egotistical way. Instead, your powerful reasoning ability and good judgment will finally expand to include yourself. Your personal life will take on greater order, and you will thereby be able to aid more people than you have in the past.

In the New Age, your mind will be used to construct ideas necessary for humankind's progress in altruistic ways, as well as designing ways to help others in general. Your nervous nature will be calmed, and you will start to take better care of yourself. You will be brought into greater balance; and with your energy being put to better use, you will be more satisfied with life in general.

Your highly-charged, affectionate nature requires expression; and the New Age, being full of change, will be made to order for your adaptive, sometimes restless, personality. You are determined to succeed; and with your ability to handle great numbers of people, you will utilize your energies to gain success in any business or profession you choose. To your success!

CAPRICORN: Your sacrificial nature will not be taken advantage of in the Age of Aquarius, for humankind will be more awakened and show greater signs of saving itself from destruction.

Governed by the planet Saturn, bringer of karma, the Divine Justice, your reality has been black and white, right or wrong. You have seen the effect of a matter as a direct result of the cause. You have almost been mired in tradition.

In the New Age you will attain a far wider vision. A middle ground will become more obvious, giving you greater balance than before. Extremes do not govern the Age of Aquarius. The past must be interblended with the future so that the present will be greater and richer.

Your charming manners and your pleasing ways will come to the fore, as well as your dynamic personality, for you will overcome the timidity which resulted from your serious nature. With balance you will have greater patience, and the smaller problems you face will not be as irritating to you as they once were. You will thereby have greater energy to apply to accomplish your goals.

The unhappiness reaped in the past, sown by your impulsiveness, will be tempered by reason and careful judgment. Listening to the golden voice within, your intuition will become second nature to you, for you will realize your first feelings of a matter carry much weight when it comes to understanding people and the ways of others.

In the New Age there will be one world, one people, and one governing body that aids Earth so that it may excel as one undivided planet. As a born leader you will be one of the primary forces behind such an accomplishment.

Being misunderstood in the past and having your loving ways unappreciated, caused you to become quite conservative and to hide your total self behind a protective shell, preventing your being sympathetic. In the New Age, your concern, your devotion, your loyal nature will be utilized to their fullest degree; and you will be greatly valued for your worth. To your recognition!

AQUARIUS: You are a true visionary, and now you can watch all that you envisioned come to fruition. You have always been decades ahead of your time, and you have been accused more than once of being an idealistic dreamer. The New Age will make all that you idealized become a reality.

Your inventive genius makes you a natural for occupations connected with scientific research. You would make an excellent scientist, sociologist, physician, inventor, or teacher. Any field that permits you to use the powers of your mind, as well as express your altruistic, humanitarian nature, is the perfect one for you.

Although you can be a great companion, lover, or friend, you are sometimes thought to be detached and cool. This is due to your highly sensitive nature. In your love relationships with the same or opposite sex, you notice the slightest inattention, even if unintentional. This can cause you to become disillusioned, permitting you to become hurt, jealous, or withdrawn. You crave love of an unconditional nature, for this is the type of love you are capable of giving. Without it, you will surround yourself with loving children and animals and create a picturesque place of retreat in which to withdraw.

The New Age will bring more love to you than you ever dreamed possible, for it is the Age of feminine consciousness, of unconditional love, of mothering, of caring, of holistic tending to the needs of all living things.

Your powers of analysis, your active mind, and your ability to create those things essential to humankind's future progress make you the most likely candidate to usher in the Age of Aquarius. Be shy no more, Child of harmony, your age is dawning; your time is here. To your Age!

PISCES: Where there has been division there will be unity. Peace and harmony will guide your decisions. Your charming, magnetic personality will blossom forth as never before, for all your reserve will disappear. You will become easily expressive and self-confident and accomplish much through your efforts.

You are a natural author, actor, actress, or religious worker. Your energies can weave wonders, permitting you to elevate others, as well as entertain. Your good powers of observations, your perceptions, your wit will help you to take your emotions in hand and permit you to make better decisions in life.

In the past, you have found it sometimes difficult to make major decisions, but this was due to the polarizing of the Pisces sign, two fish going in opposite directions. With your ability to learn quite easily, you can, through the powers of your imagination, bring others to see what it is you wish they might comprehend.

You will become far more grounded in the ways of love and human relationships, and you will be far happier than you ever thought possible, for the world of fantasy and ideals frequently bring disillusion. Utilize your brilliant memory and creative talent in your occupation, and you will be more content.

Your feelings are deep and intense; and once you are assured of a return, you can be very loving. Yet your moodiness can undermine the best of relationships. Maintain balance and do not give in to unreasonable jealousy, but choose a mate more compatible to your total self. This will be far easier in the New Age, for balance and harmony will affect all zodiacal signs and help assure you of greater compatibility.

Be patient; your great need for affection will be appeased. Do not rush headlong into relationships too soon, for your day is coming. To your creativity!

CHAPTER THREE:
INFLUENCE OTHERS THROUGH RITUAL MAGIC

Test Your Psychokinetic Powers
Building Thoughtforms
Freedom of the New Age
Set a Time for Meditation
The Proper Position for Meditation
Developing Concentration
Peace and Inner Balance
An Invocation to Diana the Moon Goddess to Enable One to Discover an Object Which One Wishes to Find or to Buy
A Ritual to Attract a Lover
A Blessing to Draw a Loved One
If it Works—Use It

LET us say that you are performing a ritual designed to make contact with a friend. While the conscious part of your mind is engaged in completing the proper steps in the ritual, your unconscious mind has been freed to make telepathic contact with your friend. Telepathically, he receives the message to call you.

To manifest precognition, the same laws apply. You would perform a ceremony designed to evoke spirit help, while in reality your own mind is doing all the work.

Once again, psychokinesis (PK) is the psi function most utilized in magic. Naturally, there is a great deal of overlap in all of these functions, but PK most clearly indicates the use of one's will in an effort to control the people and events around him.

TEST YOUR PSYCHOKINETIC POWERS

Since PK is so important to the workings of New Age magic, here is a simple test devised by W. Wilson Weir to test your psychokinetic abilities:

Get a fat piece of cork and a piece of broomstraw about two inches long. With a razor blade, make points at both ends of the broomstraw. Push one pointed end into the narrow end of the cork, so that it stands erect.

Now cut a piece of typewriter paper one quarter inch wide and one and a half inches long. Crease it lengthwise down the center. Clip the corners off one end, so that it forms a pointer. Open a large pair of scissors so that its blades support each end of the pointer. Using the scissors as a tool, lower the pointer onto the end of the straw so that it is free to pivot on it. Now very gently lower a glass tumbler over the pivoted pointer to keep drafts away.

You now have a device that is free from metal so that, whatever operates it, it cannot possibly be terrestrial magnetism--or any other kind of magnetism for that matter.

Place the device on a vibration free table. Sit before it for a few minutes with your hands clasped tightly in your lap. Now, slowly bring your right hand toward the pointer at about a 45° angle. Watch for movement of the pointer.

Take your hand away and let the pointer come to rest. Try your left hand now. Is the effect as strong?

Could the movement of the pointer be due to heat radiating from the hand? There is an easy way to disprove this. Take a piece of wood about the same diameter as a pencil and about three or four inches long. Hold it in your hand for about 20 minutes. Now move it toward the pointer.

Try the same thing with a piece of metal the same size. It may be copper, steel, aluminum or any other metal or alloy. Hold it in your hand and then move it toward the pointer.

Why should the activated wood move the pointer and the metal not? Which stores heat better, metal or wood?

If radiated heat moves the pointer, why will it not move for the substances that store heat best? Does this suggest that something other than heat moves the pointer? Isn't it apparent that whatever force is involved, wood will store it but metal will not?

Wood is a vegetable product. It was once alive. Try other vegetable products--cotton and linen, for instance. Hold them loosely in your hand to activate them and bring them to the pointer.

Do you think you could muster up enough force to move the pointer without using your hands?

Nina Kulagina of the Institute for Technical Parapsychology in Moscow is not only able to do it, but teaches others to do it as well. Dr. Stanley Krippner, formerly of the Sleep Laboratory at Maimonides Medical Center, visited Russia and brought back motion pictures of Mrs. Kulagina at work. The films show her moving small objects on a desk top. She trains others by first having them try to move the needle of a small compass.

The device you have made is much like a compass, with the added advantage that you do not fight against the Earth's magnetic force.

Try to move the pointer, not by an effort of will, but by forming a mental picture of it moving to one side or the other, as you choose. It may help if you bring your eyes quite close to the pointer. Some workers have reported that the eyes seem to emanate a psychic force.

BUILDING THOUGHTFORMS

The control of weather, the building of thoughtforms to obtain love, money, success, and influence over animals, all of this properly fits into the category of psychokinesis, and thus under the category of magic.

If you want a car and cannot afford one under your present circumstances, you can perform a ritual which includes the building of a thoughtform, and you aim it toward either receiving the car directly or receiving the money with which to purchase the car. Then you nurture this thoughtform, feed it daily with energy, and it will act as a magnet attracting a car to your garage. In this case you are applying your will to the ether, instructing your thoughtform to travel through it and bend it accordingly until the car is sitting in your driveway.

The major tools of magic, viewed from a parapsychological base, are your own mind and your own will. You decide, you act. The power is yours.

The power of the mind is vast and uncharted, yet we use only a miniscule part of it. Our imaginations are too feeble to picture for us the mighty things we can do with our minds. We do not believe we could do these things if we tried. Many feel that we should not assume these untapped powers of the mind.

FREEDOM OF THE NEW AGE

Freedom of great magnitude beckons to us, and only those fearful of the powerful responsibilities that accompany such freedom shrink from it. The ones who fear they are incapable of handling the responsibility are the ones who tell the rest of us that we dare too much. They seek to keep us bound to the same dogmas they hide behind to justify their stagnation, their refusal to grow.

The magician of the New Age should be the one who releases himself into this freedom by joyfully accepting its accompanying responsibilities. He is then allowed to develop his mind, manifesting more of its abilities in this physical life-expression, because he has proven himself capable of handling the power.

SET A TIME FOR MEDITATION

With continued practice of meditation you will learn to sharpen and discipline those two necessary factors, mind and will. And, with strengthened mind and a directed will, the powers of PK--magic--will be yours.

Set aside a certain time of the day--preferably the same time every day--and declare it to be your meditation period. Later it may become your hour for ritual work. Initially, however, 15 minutes will be all the time you will require.

If you adhere to your schedule, and, say you choose eleven o'clock in the morning, you will soon find that you subconsciously prepare for this hour. You may be engaged with some business at your office or finishing up the morning breakfast dishes, and an inner alarm will go off, telling you it is your meditation time. Also, when you become truly adept at achieving a meditational high, it will not be uncommon for you to experience a kind of "rush" at the appointed hour.

THE PROPER POSITION FOR MEDITATION

Once you have chosen a time period, settle yourself in a comfortable position, either sitting upright or lying down. The back must be straight. Make sure you sit in a position that can be maintained without some part of your body falling asleep. If you insist upon lying down, try the floor. The floor will keep your back straighter and be a better guard against falling asleep.

Your upright position may be either cross-legged, Indian yoga style, Egyptian yoga style [sitting in a chair with legs uncrossed, feet flat on the floor, hands resting on your knees] or tailor fashion.

The most important thing is that you be comfortable, and that your back be straight. Your hands should rest palms upward, flat, if you are trying to receive the power; palms up, resting on knees with tips of thumb and forefinger lightly touching, if you mean to symbolize the renunciation of self into the greater whole. The latter is a very powerful mudra of Indian yoga, and should not be used lightly.

The position of the hands for meditation is not of paramount importance. The only thing to remember is to not clasp the hands on top of the head. This interrupts the flow of power.

Once you are settled comfortably you must relax completely and empty your mind of all thoughts. This can be extremely difficult to do, but continued practice will eventually bring you to a state of complete relaxation.

AN EXERCISE FOR DEVELOPING CONCENTRATION

As a magician you will have to pay particular attention to the development of your concentration and will. Al Manning, director of the ESP Lab in Los Angeles developed the following exercise for his students:

"This is what I call the world's hardest ritual, but it is simplicity itself. We want to do six of these. The first day, five minutes; the second, ten; then fifteen, twenty, up to thirty minutes on the sixth day. By applying constructive will power you set the stage for the simplest of all rituals, which is to sit in meditation perfectly motionless. Perfectly means also with just one thought.

"To be sure this is working, use a candle--we'll leave the color up to you--as close to your nose and mouth as you can stand without the heat bothering you. The idea is to make your breathing so slow that it doesn't flicker the candle flame. If you're really motionless, then nobody would see you breathing, either. The use for this will be quite apparent as we go along.

Five minutes sounds easy, but I warn you, the first that happens is you develop an itch! You'll get lots of tests and the fun is to prove that you're stronger than the itch, the telephone, or dog or whatever wants to move you. This is part of building the ability to really use and control your own beingness."

PEACE AND INNER BALANCE

The benefits obtained from regular periods of meditation are numerous. Meditation offers you peace, inner balance, and an unruffled attitude toward all that comes your way. All of these benefits are valuable to the practicing magician. They give a solid foundation from which to sally forth into the unknown. They also provide an ethical basis from which to determine the proper uses of psychokinetic powers.

Magic, then, is the special application of the psi functions of telepathy, clairvoyance, precognition, and psychokinesis. These powers manifest from the altered state of consciousness recognized by science as the state marked by high production of alpha brain waves, as measured by an electroencephalograph. Of equal importance is a strong, disciplined will.

These are the mechanics of magic, the mind principles that must be understood before any of the rituals make sense. To achieve the results you desire, and to be able to repeat them, you must understand and actively apply the mechanism behind the magic.

AN INVOCATION TO DIANA, THE MOON GODDESS, TO ENABLE ONE TO DISCOVER AN OBJECT WHICH ONE WISHES TO FIND OR TO BUY.

'Tis---(Name of day) now, and at an early hour
I fain would turn good fortune to myself,
Firstly at home and then what I go forth,
And with the aid of the beautiful *Diana*
I pray for luck ere I do leave this house!

Three drops of oil are now required. These are given in propitiation to Diana with the supplication that she will remove any evil influence which might be lurking about.

Sprinkle the oil (use vegetable oil, baby oil, it doesn't matter) one drop at a time onto your left wrist. As you do so, visualize the object that you wish to find or buy.

Then say aloud:
Then well contented
I will go forth to roam,
Because I shall be sure that with thy aid
I shall discover ere I return
Some----(whatever object you desire)
And at a moderate price.

Conclude with an additional plea to enchant the owner of the desired object into parting with it "at little cost" to you. Today's modern competitive supermarket shopper should certainly see the advantages of such a charm.

A RITUAL TO ATTRACT A LOVER

Here is a simple ritual that an occult teacher named Jeanyne uses when she wants a date with a particular man:

Step one: The first thing I do is prepare my room and myself for the ritual.

Preparing the room usually means choosing the proper incense, lighting it and the candles, filling my vessels—one with earth and one with salt water. It also includes locking the door to my house and taking the phone off the hook [there is nothing worse than the sudden ringing of the telephone to jolt you out of trance].

Preparing myself means making sure I am wearing loose, comfortable clothes, that I am reasonably clean. Then I seat myself on the floor before my altar paraphernalia and place myself in an altered state of consciousness, or light trance state.

When I am confident that I am tuned into the Creative Forces, I proceed.

Step two: To further assist with my attunement, I usually chant at this point. The idea of chanting is to get the body vibrating at one pitch, then raise the chant by one whole step and so vibrate the body at the higher frequency. It is also a focal point for concentration. It gives my conscious mind something to dwell on while I am emptying my mind of all extraneous thoughts.

Chants are very personal things; you will have to discover which ones turn you on. I like the Hindu "Om Mane Padme Hum," lingering on the "Hum" part. I also like the Edgar Cayce chant: "Arrr-eee-ooo-uuu-mmm." When it really starts to rattle inside your head, you know you are doing it correctly.

Step three: At this point I cease my chanting and soak up its effects. This is the time for motionless attunement, perfect calm, and complete confidence in the outcome of the ritual.

Step four: Keeping the same level of concentration that has been achieved, I next develop the specific thing I want.

I put forth a logical argument in favor of my desire, in this case explaining why I wish to go on this particular date, and why I have chosen the particular person in mind as the one best suited to take me.

It is a process of persuading myself, to further deepen my confidence in what I am doing. In the process of this monologue with myself I try to boil down my argument into one essential phrase, which I then repeat over and over again.

Step five: The following is quoted directly from Al Manning:

"Then comes the act of building the thoughtform. Hold your hands about six inches apart with the palms facing each other. Will the energy to flow between them and feel it. Then visualize a triangle from your heart and brow center to the center of the thoughtform [between your hands] and invite the help of the conscious and unconscious parts of your being."

Step six: At this point I take the essential words of my desire, the ones I arrived at in step four, and I begin to chant them into the thoughtform growing between my outstretched hands.

Frequently I call upon ancient dieties to add power to the chant. When, as in this case, I want a man to take me somewhere, I call upon Isis, Ishtar, Diana, Venus, or Aphrodite. It is essential in your chant that you state your desire *will* manifest. Speak as though it is *already happening* and include your thanks, accordingly.

Step seven: Now comes the important step of breathing life into your thoughtform. This is difficult to get the knack of, at first, but it is actually very easy.

Instead of breathing with *my* body, I breath out and in *as the thoughtform*. While still concentrating on the triangle of energy and while still chanting, I subtly shift my breathing *into* the thoughtform growing between my hands. My hands are gently pulled in and out by the suction of this strange respiration. I can feel it pulsating.

Step eight: When I am sure that I have infused this thoughtform with a life of its own, I instruct it to fulfill its mission and serve me well. I surround it mentally with protection and rise to my feet, still holding the thoughtform carefully.

When I am standing I release the thoughtform into the air, as though I am freeing an imprisoned bird. Then I stand in the star position, repeating the instructions for it to fulfill my desire. I bless it, put it from my mind, and wait for the phone to ring.

In this ritual I am toning up my concentrative powers with the chanting, emptying my mind of all thought, achieving a meditative state through which the phenomena can manifest, and employing the basic psi functions of man.

In steps four, six and seven, I usually visualize the thing I want as already taking place, thus using some of the principles of clairvoyance. Also, the channels used in telepathy make the initial contact.

Once the target has been reached, however, psychokinesis takes over. What else should suddenly make this man want to take me to a movie or the theater?

I should add that it helps to be as specific as possible. One night I could not decide between four eligible guys, so I instructed the thoughtform to go to each and choose the one for whom it was most convenient. That night I went to the movie with one, but the next night I had to turn down two of the others because I was already going out with the fourth!

You can see from the ritual, though, how much time is given to achieving the proper mental state, and you can judge the priorities from there. This higher level of consciousness must be reached before you can ever hope effectively to practice magic. The rewards are all circular: magic uses psychic abilities; psychic abilities manifest from altered, or alpha state of consciousness; alpha state is the singular medium through which magic works.

A BLESSING TO DRAW A LOVED ONE

Focus your thoughts on Diana, huntress of the night, goddess of the Moon. Next, visualize your loved one and say aloud:

> D*iana, bella* D*iana!*
> (Diana, beautiful Diana!)
> C*he tanto bella e buona siei,*
> (Who are indeed as good as beautiful,)
> By all the worship I have given thee...
> ...I do implore thee aid me in my love!
> What thou wilt 'tis true
> Thou canst ever do:

Now in your own words, as if in earnest prayer, ask for specifics and beseech Aradia, daughter of Diana, to go the bedside of the desired one and to whisper to him (her) of your great love. Then say:

> And make her (him) then come to me and to my room,

And when she/he once has entered it, I pray
Then she/he may ever be
As beautiful as e'er she/he was before,
And may I then make love to her/him until
Our souls with joy are fully satisfied.

Terminate with the prayer that the enchanted person remain under your spell of love. Pledge to Diana that you will never abuse or mistreat the object of your desire.

ASSEMBLING YOUR ALTAR

The materials for rituals traditionally include the altar and the magic circle. Upon the altar rest the tools to be used for the particular ceremony.

All materials should be new, but with the proper consecration, old, used items can be used.

The occultist Jeanyne tells us that her own array of tools includes an incense burner purchased by a friend at one of the Arab markets in Saudi Arabia.

"This burner is of undeterminate age and belonged to only the gods know whom. I feel confident, though, that I have removed any negative vibrations from it, and that it has been made new for my purposes. It lends a touch of the exotic to my altar.

"Your vessels for the elements can suit your own fancy. I usually vacillate between silver cups and pottery. My chalice is earthenware, and my candlesticks, iron. I usually choose purple candles; although for certain ceremonies I will substitute green or blue." Jeanyne continued, explaining:

> An altar is something you will want to construct very early in your ritual work. My own consists of a plank of wood balanced upon a cement block. The altar is alternately left bare or covered with Belgium linen.
>
> I leave my altar up in my bedroom, but some of you may have cause to keep yours tucked away in a closet, hauling it out only when you are alone or planning a specific ritual. In this case, since the altar should also be a consecrated item, you should perform a ritual for consecration each time you set it up.

CHAPTER FOUR:
DETERMINE YOUR MAGIC NUMBERS FOR SUCCESS ON YOUR LIFEPATH

Your Life-Path Number
Your Day Number
Your Soul-Urge Number
Life Expression Numbers of the Stars (as examples of how to do your own)
Charles Bronson
Linda Gray
George Peppard
William Shatner
Larry Hagman
Racquel Welch
The Law of Oneness

IN the late 1960s, I met a remarkable woman named Marguerite Haymes, who had combined the principles of astrology, numerology, Yoga, the Indian Vedas, the ancient wisdom of the Egyptians, and the Kabbala into a "science of numbers" that she termed "Unitology." The mother of Dick Haymes who had been a popular singer in the 1940s and 1950s, Marguerite had also enjoyed a career as a singer, as well as a leader in the world of Paris fashion.

Marguerite told me of her teacher in the esoteric mysteries, a Master Teacher named Athena, who taught her the "Unique Principle," that each individual is equipped with a different assignment. Each individual assignment has been designed to fulfill a destiny, and each of us is created with equal opportunity to direct his or her own fate.

Maurice Jacquet, High Priest of the European order of Rosicrucians, taught her "... the spiritual interpretation of numbers and their mathematical accuracy in relation to music and its interpretation in any form," Marguerite said. It was through this man that she began to realize the great necessity for the coordination or "Unitology" of mind, body and spirit.

Eventually this phase of her active life came to a close and again it was time for a change. Returning to America she began to teach modern singing. Soon she was known as a "star-maker," with graduates in every facet of the entertainment field.

"This section of my Life-Path lasted for over 20 years. I loved it. Being privileged to guide youth through music is a sheer joy. I grew and learned through my students while still doing research in the occult sciences. During this phase of my life I was led to my last earthly teacher, Paramahansa Yogananda, a high priest and Master of Eastern Philosophy."

From Yogananda she learned all that she was "supposed to know" before he passed on.

The great Yogi's Life-Path was a nine, and thus his destiny was the brotherhood of man.

Accordingly, Marguerite found that her search for additional teachings or teachers had subsided, while the continuing search within had been "revealing beyond words." Her own numbers for this last cycle are 11 and 22--decreeing that she will "enlighten the minds and hearts of my fellow travelers to the joy of living through the potential of their inner power."

By this time you well may ask, "What is this inner power and how may I tap it?"

YOUR LIFE-PATH NUMBER

Marguerite Haymes set down the principles and mechanics by which she governed her life. All that humans are capable of experiencing, she maintained, can be reduced to the digits one through nine.

These single numbers are derived from the simplification of all combinations of numbers to their basic essence. This essence then vibrates through the single digit.

Beyond this cycle of nine, though, are the two Master Numbers 11 and 22. These never are reduced to single digits.

A personal chart in Unitology will include four major numbers. These four are: the Life-Path Number, the Day, the Expression, and the Soul-Urge Number. The first and most important number, the Life-Path number, derives from one's birth date.

Let us take the following birthdate for purposes of illustration:

```
March 29, 1922
3     11     14
3 + 11 + 5 = 19
            1 + 9 = 1ø = 1
```

The number has been found in this manner: March, the third month, gives us the number three. The day gives us 2 + 9 = 11. 1 + 9 + 2 + 2 = 14. Three reduces no further. Eleven does not reduce, being a Master Number. Fourteen (1 + 4) reduces to five; 3 + 11 + 5 = 19, 1 + 9 = 10 reduces to 1.

The number one, then is the most important number in this person's life. It is his destiny, which he cannot change, but which he does have the ability to direct.

From this number, he may determine his potential, his hidden aptitudes, talents and desires. According to Marguerite his number one "symbolizes his rate of vibration--his frequency--indicating his specific 'assignment' in life."

Here, then, according to Unitology, is the specific meaning for each number, with the key words to the Life-Path number indicated:

1 - Key word **Individualization.**

The number one person is one who always stands on his own two feet. He is independent and needs to be, as he tends to be the oak that shelters multitudes.

He must strengthen his own powers and use his own brain to devise original methods; in short, he must create. He must control and direct his body, mind and spirit to the utmost efficiency.

He should accept no limitations, yet he must learn to cooperate without losing his individuality.

2 - Key word **Adaptability.**

A person with the number two will naturally follow the lead of others. Those with this number become excellent diplomats, peacemakers and go-betweens.

Here, as opposed to the number one, the attraction is to groups, to communities. The number two is a perfect wife, for all other numbers are compatible with her.

This person is a good mixer, enjoys serving others with love and consideration and is sensitive to rhythm and music.

3 - Key word **Self-expression.**

A person on this Life-Path is one who has discovered the joy of living. He will tend to find his opportunities on the lighter side of life, in circulating and socializing.

An artistic environment is best for the three personality as he always is seeking expression through writing, speaking or art.

These people are invaluable at social gatherings and generally are considered "the life of the party."

4 - Key word **Organization.**

These people are the buliders, those who start with a firm foundation and build something of lasting importance. People who are "Fours" serve patiently and dependably and are capable of great achievements.

Just as four is the number of Earth, so are the people down-to-earth. They do the job at hand, striving to perfect the form of the thing before them.

5 - Key word **Freedom.**

Those with the number five as their Life-Path must be prepared for frequent, unexpected change and variety.

Five personalities do a lot of traveling and learn to understand all classes and conditions of people; they are without racial prejudice.

Five people always are seeking the new and progressive. Their big challenge is to learn to discard judiciously. These people grow only by adapting themselves to change and uncertainty.

Interestingly the Life-Path of the United States is a five.

6 - The key word **Adjustment.**

These are the responsible ones because six is the number of devotional impersonal love. They serve quietly, cheerfully and efficiently, applying the law of balance to adjust inharmonious conditions.

People often come to the six person for material or spiritual aid and he must always be ready to give it.

Some persons with a six Life-Path are musically endowed, but their real love is for the home and the harmony therein.

7 - Key word **Wisdom.**

Seven is a "Cosmic" number--related to the seven planets, seven days of the week, seven colors and seven notes on the musical scale. Things and opportunities are brought to the seven person, without his active seeking.

Seven is the number of the mental analyst. Those with this number seek answers. They should use their mental abilities to probe the deep mysteries and hidden truths of the universe. They are unconcerned with material goods, for they know that by applying spiritual laws they will prosper.

These people need rest and time to study and know themselves. They are potential mystics and tend to need life theories to guide them.

8 - Key word **Material Freedom.**

Those bearing the number eight in their Life-Path

are the practical people of the material world. They usually want and love power and success.

Those "Number Eights" are willing to work and should be ready to take any opportunity to demonstrate their efficiency and executive ability.

Eight is the number associated with large corporations and organizations. It is a powerful number. Like electricity, it has the ability to bring light for the benefit of humanity or it has the power to electrocute.

9 - Key word **Universality.**

This is the number representing the Brotherhood of Man. This is a difficult path, as it requires complete humanitarianism.

Those under this vibration must be prepared to give up all personal desire and ambitions. They will find their greatest opportunities with emotional, artistic and inspirational people, as nine is the highest vibration of the artist.

Number nine operates under the Law of Fulfillment, and its appeal is to the all-inclusive, to the many.

11 - A Master Number: Key word **Revelation.**

This is the dreamer, the visionary, the one who receives his ideals intuitively.

Those on this vibration are on a higher plane than the strictly material and their destiny is to reveal something new and uplifting to the world.

The "Number Eleven" is the messenger, the spokesman or broadcaster.

22 - A Master Number: Key word **Material Master.**

This is the practical idealist who takes the ideal of the 11 and puts it to practical use. The 22 is the master on the material plane, concerned with the benefit and progress of mankind.

A 22 readily takes on international proportions and conceives philanthropic plans.

The appeal on the path of the 22 is to the masses for their improvement, expansion and growth.

Before we examine Unitology further, it is necessary to include the negative aspects, or the lower end of the vibrational poles, of the above numbers. Briefly:

1 - Key word **Self.**
2 - Key word **Self-effacement.**
3 - Key word **Superficiality.**
4 - Key word **Square.**
5 - Key word **Self-indulgence.**
6 - Key word **Tyranny.**

7 - Key word **Withdrawal.**
8 - Key word **Demander.**
9 - Key word **Egocentricity.**
11- Key word **Fanaticism.**
22- Key word **Promoter.**

Once you have the basic interpretation of each number, Marguerite said, you might use them to figure out your own chart. After the Life-Path number has been determined, you may continue to make your own chart by obtaining the Day number-vibration.

YOUR DAY

Going back to our previous example of March 29, 1922, the Day number is reached by simplifying 29 to 11, which is, as a Master Number, not reduced further. The Day number always works in unison with the Life-Path number for directing the purpose of its expression. In determining an individual chart, one should go back and read the meanings of these two numbers and see how they complement each other or strike contrasts.

For the next two major numbers it is necessary to leave the birth date and go on to the actual name.

A name is very important, according to the precepts of Unitology, as it is concerned with **sound**, a direct manifestation of vibration. Therefore, since each letter of every alphabet has its distinctive sound, it follows that each letter would have its own distinctive number. Using the one to nine cycle it is imperative to establish the essence of the number.

The graph which follows, with a name given as an example, shows how to arrive at the number vibration.

```
            1 2 3 4 5 6 7 8 9
            A B C D E F G H I
            J K L M N O P Q R
            S T U V W X Y Z
```

Example:

```
   M A R Y      L O U      H A Y E S
   4 1 9 7      3 6 3      8 1 7 5 1
     21          12          22
      3           3           4
```

10 (10) = 1

The one is the number of Mary Lou Hayes' expression.

Expression relates to the outer self. It relates to the character in general, the personality. Referring back to the basic explanation of the number vibration, a one would make "Mary" an independent person with a will of her own. She would have the ability to lead her own life and stand on her own two feet.

YOUR SOUL URGE NUMBER

The fourth and final major number is the Soul-Urge number. Unitology finds this by totaling the number of the vowels of one's name.

Using Mary's name again we get the numbers 1 + 7 + 6 + 1 + 7 + 5. By totaling and simplifying these we arrive at the final digit of three. This number represents Mary's Soul-Urge, her inner self. It expresses her real potential, longings and hidden talents. As a three, her Soul-Urge is to give and to express joy, to love all people, all creatures, all aspects of life.

"As your knowledge of unitology increases," Marguerite said, "you should start noting interesting comparisons between your own chart and the charts of those connected with your present Life-Path. Learn to use numbers. Apply them to your everyday tasks and your thoughts surrounding those tasks. Be willing to tune in to your own vibrational path and flow with it.

"You will be amazed at how much easier things will become. In essence, you will stop fighting yourself and learn to direct Universal laws, operating at a much higher frequency, into your life."

LIFE EXPRESSION NUMBERS OF THE STARS

Before you set to work to determine your own Life-Path, Life Expression, Day, and Soul Urge numbers, you might find it interesting to use some of your favorite television and motion picture performers as further illustrations.

For example, tough guy *Charles Bronson* might surprise you. His birthname of Charles Buchinsky gives him a Life Expression number of 11, a Master Number which places him on a higher vibrational plane than the strictly material. As a youth, it is likely that he received his ideals on an intuitive level. By changing his name to Bronson, he became a 1, thereby, no doubt, increasing his personal emphasis on individuality.

His Life Path number (November 3, 1922) is a 2, providing him with the adaptability that is so necessary to one's becoming an effective actor. His Soul Urge number is a 5, letting us know that his inner self yearns most for freedom and the quest for the new and progressive.

Combine all of the above with his Day number of 3, self-expression, and we see a pattern profile of adaptability, creativity, and intuition that blends into a sensitive man who just happens to be effective playing action roles.

Linda Gray, who was born on September 12, 1940, has a Life Path number of 8, the electrical number of material freedom, thereby preparing her from birth to essay the role of the wife of success-hungry J. R. Ewing on *Dallas*.

Her Life Expression number of 1 indicates a person who has learned to cooperate without losing her individuality—certainly a necessary attribute of an ensemble actor.

Linda Gray has the Soul Urge number of 11, a Master Number. This tells us that in her inner self she is a dreamer, a visionary, who receives a great many intuitive insights. And since she also has a Day number of 3, for self-expression, Linda Gray will always function best in an artistic environment.

The A-Team's confident leader, *George Peppard* (October 1, 1928), has a Life Path number of 4, thus indicating that he would be a builder and a leader in whatever area of life he chose to express himself. His Day number of 1 reveals his refusal to accept any limitations imposed by others.

With Peppard's life Expression number of 7, we can readily see why he has so often portrayed detectives and police investigators in his motion pictures and television series. Seven is the number of the mental analyst who loves to probe deep mysteries. In his *Banacek* series, Peppard played a brilliant insurance investigator who found no mystery too difficult to solve.

Peppard's Soul Urge number is also a 4, so we know that his inner self desires always to perfect the form of whatever challenge lies before him.

William Shatner, the bold Captain Kirk of *Star Trek* and the brave policeman of *T. J. Hooker*, has the Master Number 11 as his Life Expression number. Shatner has it as his destiny to reveal something new and uplifting to the world, thus qualifying him to play roles that have him soaring to cosmic dimensions. His Life Expression is the number of the messenger.

Shatner's Day number of 4 (March 22, 1931) intensifies his leadership qualities. His Life Path number of 3, that of self-expression, tells us that he will only be contented when he is seeking fulfillment through his craft of communication. His Soul Urge number 8 gives him the inner power to take any opportunity to demonstrate his efficiency and his executive abilities.

When we examine Larry Hagman's numerical scan (September 21, 1931), we can readily seen that he is not really as mean and conniving as the tricky J. R. Ewing whom he impersonates on *Dallas*. Since both Day and Soul Urge numbers total 3, the digit of self-expression, we note that he is an artistic sort who enjoys being friendly and sociable.

Hagman's Life Expression number is a 1, the numeral of the individual who is always prepared to stand on his own two feet. He, too, as his co-star Linda Gray, has learned to cooperate with others without losing his individuality.

And we cannot fail to notice that both of these actors, who portray husband and wife on the highly successful *Dallas* television series, have an 8 as their Life Path number. As we have already seen, 8 is the number of material freedom, the number of those who love power and success.

Racquel Welch (September 5, 1942) who has long been considered a "10" by male moviegoers, is just that--except, as we pointed out, the zero does not remain in our system of analysis. Interestingly, though, Racquel's birth name, Tejada, as well as her professional name, add up to 10; and her Soul Urge number totals a 10. But once we reduce them, of course, they are all the number 1.

We must say, then, that Racquel (Tejada) Welch in both her Life Expression and her Soul Urge is revealed as a person who has a great desire to control and to direct her body, mind and spirit to the utmost efficiency. She is one who must always be independent and be seeking to improve herself.

Her Day number of 5 emphasizes her need for freedom, her wish to travel widely, and her striving to be always adaptable. Racquel Welch's Life Path number 3 underlines her need to be a communicator, functioning best in an artistic environment.

THE LAW OF ONENESS

"We must obey the Laws coming from above us, but on our own plane we must govern and give the orders," Marguerite Haymes once said to me. "And yet, in so doing, we form a part of the Whole...the Oneness. Once we know this teaching, we fall in with the Law and operate it instead of being used by it.

We are truly magnetic when we are on our own vibrant mental wavelength. When this is understood, it is easy to see how so-called miracles are performed."

Kihief

Frances first received angelic contact when she was but a child of five. She has since maintained regular interaction with multidimensional beings.

CHAPTER FIVE:
ALIGNING YOURSELF WITH ANGELS AND GUIDES

The Seven Major Spirits
The Revelation of Hermes-Thoth
The three Angelic Hierarchies
Spirits Are Here to Help Us
The Word of Power
Enochian Magical Words
Abracadabra!
The Magical Circle
Solomon's Seal
Ancient Grimoires
Solomon's Circle
Spirit Guides to do Your Bidding
The High Self
Direction the Low Self

THE SEVEN MAJOR SPIRITS

THERE were seven major planetary spirits, or Archangels, whom the medieval magicians were interested in contacting: **Raphael, Gabriel, Camael, Michael, Zadikel, Haniel, Zaphkiel.** One of the original sources of such instruction comes from the great Egyptian Magi and master of the occult, Hermes-Thoth. In the fragments remaining from one of his treatises, the *Pymander* (divine thought), Hermes described the revelation he had been given regarding this matter.

One night, Hermes saw a shimmering vision begin to form in the darkness. As it became clearer, this luminescence took the form of a perfectly formed, colossal man of great beauty.

THE REVELATION OF HERMES-THOTH

Gently, it spoke to Hermes: "O son of Earth, I come to give thee strength, for thou lovest justice and thou seekest after truth. I am Pymander, the thought of the All-Powerful: make a wish, and it shall be granted thee."

"Lord," rejoined Hermes-Thoth, "give me a ray of thy divine knowledge."

Pymander granted the wish, and Hermes was immediately inundated with wondrous visions, all beyond human comprehension and imagination. After the imagery had ceased, the blackness surrounding Hermes grew terrifying. A harsh and discordant voice boomed through the ether, creating a chaotic tempest of roaring winds and thunderous explosions. The mighty and terrible voice left Hermes filled with awe.

"It seemed to me (the text of the P*ymander* reads) that this great voice was the voice of the vanished Light, and from it came the Word of God. This Word seemed to be borne on a current of celestial water whose coolness I could feel, and from it rose a clear, pure flame that dissolved into the air.

"'From the All-Powerful come **seven spirits** who move in seven circles; and in these circles are all the beings that compose the universe; and the action of the seven Spirits in their circles is called Fate, and these circles themselves are enclosed in the divine Thought that permeates them eternally.

"'God has committed to the seven Spirits the governing of the elements and the creation of their combined products. But He created man in His own image, and, pleased with this image, has given him power over terrestrial nature.

"'God desires that every man should learn to know himself for what he is, and to distinguish his superior and invisible being from the visible form, which is only the shell. When he has recognized the duality of his creation, he no longer allows himself to be seduced by the charm of impermanent things; his thought has no other aim but to seek and pursue, across the infinite, the absolute beauty whose contemplation is the sovereign good promised to his rehabilitated mind.

"'The man who triumphs over sensual temptations increases his mental faculties; God gives him his measure of light in proportion to his merits, and progressively allows him to penetrate the most profound mysteries of nature.

"'That man, on the contrary, who succumbs to the temptations of the flesh falls gradually under the power of the fatal laws that govern the elements and condemns himself to perpetual ignorance, which is the death of the spirit.

"'Happy is the son of earth who has kept pure the image of God and has not defaced it or darkened it with the veil of ignoble concupiscence. When the hour comes for him to leave his world, his body is indeed given up to the realm of matter; but his spirit, freed from the shell that time has worn away, rises into the seven concentric circles that envelop the terrestrial system.

"'In the circle of the **Moon**, he recognizes his immortality; in **Mercury**, he feels his insensibility; in **Venus**, he clothes himself again in innocence; in the **Sun**, he is given the strength to bear without difficulty the rays of the divine splendour; in **Mars**, he learns humility; in **Jupiter**, he takes possession of the treasures of an intelligence made divine, and in **Saturn**, he sees the truth of all things in its unchangeable beauty.

"'Beyond the circles lies the Infinity of Worlds, that goes with him in his pilgrimage from heaven to heaven towards the supreme God whom he approaches ceaselessly...'"

It is these seven superior spirits of the Egyptian system, acting as intermediaries between God and men, that the Brahmans of ancient India called the seven **Devas**, that in Persia were called the seven **Amaschaspands**, that in Chaldea were called the seven **Great Angels**, that in Jewish Kabbalism are called the seven **Archangels**.

THE THREE ANGELIC HIERARCHIES

Dionysius the pseudo-Areopagite prepared a treatise for Westerners, reconciling the Christian hierarchy of celestial spirits with the traditions of Hermes. He classified the angels into three hierarchies, each subdivided into three orders.

First Hierarchy - Seraphim, Cherubim, and Thrones
Second Hierarchy - Dominions, Powers, and Authorities [Virtues]
Third Hierarchy - Principalities Archangels, and Angels.

The following is a description of the seven principal angels from the Heptameron, or Magical Elements, taken from the *Fourth Book of Occult Philosophy*, translated into English by Robert Turner in 1655:

Of **Michael and the other spirits of Sunday** it is written that: "Their nature is to procure Gold, Gemmes, Carbuncles, Riches; to cause one to obtain favour and benevolence; to dissolve the enmities of men; to raise men to honors; to carry or take away infirmities."

Of **Gabriel and the other spirits of Monday**: "Their nature is to give silver; to convey things from place to place; to make horses swift, and to disclose the secrets of persons both present and future."

Of **Samuel and the other spirits of Tuesday**: "Their nature is to cause wars, mortality, death and combustions; and to give two thousand Soldiers at a time; to bring death, infirmities or health," and so on for **Raphael, Sachiel, Anael, Cassiel**, and their colleagues.

These seven are said to govern the portion of the astral system of which our planet is the center. Each of these portions consists of the seven orbits through which pass the Moon, Mercury, Venus, the Sun, Mars, Jupiter, and Saturn. These planets are considered the thrones, or centers of influence, of the seven superior spirits or Archangels, each one of which has command over one of the angelic legions.

SPIRITS ARE HERE TO HELP US

These spirits are more perfect in essence than man, and they are here to help us. They work out the pattern of ordeals that each human being must pass through, and they give an account of our actions to God after we pass from the physical plane.

They cannot, however, interfere in any way with our free will, which always must make the choice between good and evil. In their capacity to help, though, they can be called upon to assist us in various ways. It is these archangels, then, that the magician evokes in his ceremonies.

THE WORD OF POWER

Accompanying the concept of the planetary spirits, or Archangels, was something the Egyptians called **hekau**, or the word of power. The word of power, when spoken, released a vibration capable of evoking spirits.

The most powerful **hekau** for calling up a specific spirit in Ceremonial Magic is that spirit's name.

"To name is to define," cried Count Cagliostro, a famous occultist of the eighteenth century. And, to the magicians of the Middle Ages, to know the name of a spirit was to be able to command its presence.

ENOCHIAN MAGICAL WORDS

"The actual evocation begins with the use of pentacles and the chanting of the appropriate words", according to occult scholar Edward Costain. "These vary from spirit to spirit. Often the chants are made up by the magician himself. Frequently they involve the use of words of power. These are words which, by their very sounds, exert a strong emotional effect.

A famous example is: *Eca, zodocare, iad, goho.Torzodu odo kilale qaa! Zodacare, od sodameranu! Zodorje lape zodiredo ol noco mada, das iadapiel! Ilas! Hoatache iaida!*

The words are from the Enochian Language, believed

by magicians and other occultists to pre-date Sanskrit. They translate as follows:

"Move, therefore, and show yourselves! Open the mysteries of your creation! Be friendly unto me for I am servant of the same, your God; the true worshipper of the Highest."

Other words, more appropriate to Hathor are *Athorebalo* (Thou goddess of beauty and love), *Aeoou* (Lady of the Western Gate of Heaven), *Mriodom* (thou, the Sea, the Abode), and *Ma* (mother of Truth).

Quoting again from Costain: In all chanting and recitation, the impact of a group is far more impressive than that of a single voice. A group also lends itself to litanies. Needless to say, such a group must be of individuals of like dedication.

All barbarous words of power are vibrated. That is, they are chanted as from the diaphragm, slowly and loudly. The hymns are sung slowly with emphasis on cadences.

When properly performed, such rituals have a powerful impact on the emotions. This is heightened by a measured walking around the inside of the circle, and dancing. For the latter, a simple two-step is used, though, as a matter of fact, the waltz is supposed to have derived from a magical step.

There are minor rituals that employ symbolism for various purposes. One is the Ritual of The Pentagram. It is used for three different purposes.

First, as an invoking ritual at the beginning of any rite.

Secondly, as a banishing ritual to cut off the magical power after any rite.

And, finally, as a prayer against obsessing and disturbing thoughts.

To perform the ritual, the magician uses a steel dagger when he can. If he cannot, he uses the thumb of his right hand, clenched between index and second fingers, as a pointer. He makes a sign of a cross with arms of equal length, corresponding to the four elements, and asserting his identity as a magician.

Touching his forehead, he says **Ateh**--(to you). Touching his breast, he says **Malkuth**--(the Earth). Touching his right shoulder, he says **Geburah**--(the Might). Touching his left shoulder, he says **Gedulah**--(the splendor). Now he brings both hands together before his breast and says **La Alam**--(Forever). With his dagger held between his palms, point uppermost, he says **Amen**.

Now, facing east, he uses his dagger--or thumb--to trace a pentagram in the air before him. He begins at its uppermost point and makes a star in one continuous line, going to the lower left hand angle first. He puts the dagger at the center of the pentagram and vibrates the Name **YHVH** - spoken as **Yod He Vau He**.

The ritual is repeated in the directions of south, west, and north. Using respectively the names **Adonai**, **Eheieh**, and **Agla**.

Facing east again, the magician brings his dagger or thumb to the center of the original pentagram, then extends his arms in the form of a cross and says:

"Before me stands **Raphael**. Behind me stands **Gabriel**. At my right hand stands **Michael**. At my left hand stands **Auriel**...Before me flames the pentagram. Behind me shines the six-pointed star."

Once more the magical cross is made.

This ritual is performed before beginning any magical ceremony or act.

ABRACADABRA!

The most famous magic word of all is not just part of a stage magician's patter. It was recorded as an *ancient* spell as early as the third century. Some scholars aver that the charm goes back to the Chaldeans of Babylonia and that the pronunciation of the word translates almost precisely into modern English.

According to some authorities, the charm was used to lower fevers. As the afflicted one whittled away at the word, so would the fever be removed from his body. To assure a speedy recovery, the charm was written on a piece of parchment and hung about the patient's neck by a cord. The word is to be said and rapidly repeated in this manner:

```
ABRACADABRA
ABRACADABR
ABRACADAB
ABRACADA
ABRACAD
ABRACA
ABRAC
ABRA
ABR
AB
A
```

THE MAGICAL CIRCLE

A spirit could not be called without the magician first taking steps to protect himself. Should he not do this, his soul would be in danger. Protection took the form of talismans, seals, sigils, special powdered concoctions, and, most importantly, the magic circle. As long as the magician stood **within** the the magic circle, he was invulnerable to whatever he managed to call up.

A variety of circles were used. Sometimes a triple circle was drawn, the diameter of each concentric circle being six inches less than the one surrounding it. The outermost circle was marked at four equidistant points for north, south, east, and west. Hebrew words were written at each point: A*gial* at the eastern, T*zabaoth* at the southern, J*hvh* at the western, and A*dhby* at the northern. Between each of these points a pentacle, or five-pointed star, was drawn.

The magician placed his brazier of lighted charcoal at the eastern point, in the smallest circle. Then his altar, its center plumb with the center of the brazier, was devised. Upon the altar were the ritual tools, including salt water, incense, candles, and herbs appropriate to his specific undertaking. Lighted candles would also be placed around the outside circle. Each tool was carefully consecrated and wrapped in white linen.

In the circle with him, the magician would have prepared the proper talismans. Inscribed also within the circle were the seals of the spirits to be evoked.

A triangle is drawn to the side of the magic circle, and it is in this triangle that the spirit is to manifest. The magician then commences with the conjuration, the first order of business being the evocation of the magician's own guardian spirit. This is a further assurance of protection. Then the evocation of the planetary spirit is attempted.

SOLOMON'S SEAL

Still other rites demand that the magician draw a circle containing Solomon's seal (Star of David) with a rectangle superimposed over it, a cross within the center diamond formed by the seal.

Solomon's seal was especially recommended for summoning air spirits. According to Peter of Abano (an occult author who lived from 1250 to 1318), this summoning should take place when the moon is waxing.

Abano also recommended the inscription of four concentric

circles for the invocation of good spirits. This should be done in the first hour of a Sunday in springtime.

The names inscribed in the circles were **Varcan**, the Lord's king-angel of the air, and **Tus, Andas,** and **Cynabel**, who are the Lord's holy ministers. The highest angels of Sunday, according to Abano, are **Michael, Dardiel,** and **Huratapal.** The north wind carries these angels, and they can be invoked by magical ceremonies employing incense made of red sanders.

There are other instructions for circles and signs contained in the various magic books, or **grimoires**, of the Middle Ages.

SOLOMON'S CIRCLE

The most revered book of all is *La Clavicul-de Salomon*, reputedly written by King Solomon of Judea. The book is for the most part a collection of invocations, magical seals, and secret formulae culled from many practicing sorcerers.

In manuscript No. 2350, *Bibliotheque de l'Arsenal*, there is a diagram of a circle with the words: "Note that nothing can be done to invoke spirits without a circle."

This circle is to be drawn with a diameter of nine feet, using the consecrated knife, or *athame*. Inscribed in the circle are many Greek and Hebrew names, as well as the oft-repeated mystical word, *agla*. *Agla* is an abbreviation used by the Rabbis, formed by the initial letters in the phrase, *"Athah gabor leolam, Adonai,"* or "Thou art mighty forever, O Lord."

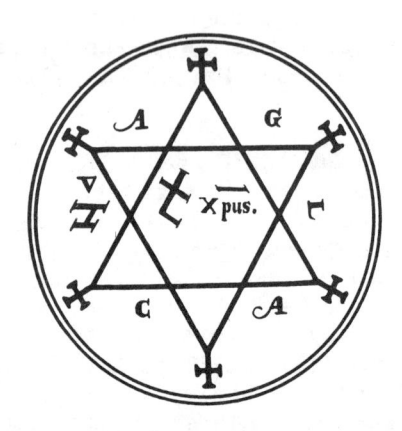

CHAPTER SIX:
HOW TO CONTACT BENEVOLENT SPIRITS

Do not Rush Spirit Contact
Be Serious
Set a Regular Time
Complete Darkness Is Not Necessary
Expectancy
Clairvoyance
Crystal Gazing
Automatic Writing
Gathering A Group
Sender/Receiver
The Circle
The Seance
Spirit Manifestations
The Medium
Trance
Messages
Physical Phenomena

FRANCES has communicated with the spirit world ever since she was a small child. The only problem she has is that she finds it difficult to distinguish between the physically living and the physically dead. To her, an entity is an entity.

Sometimes we play a little game in which I give her the name of an individual. She describes that person perfectly, often down to the smallest detail.

Then I ask her, is that person alive or dead?

Very often, she has to go rather deep within to tell me that answer. Her stream-of-consciousness that was flowing so quickly begins to dam up a bit until her guides can inform her of the present physical state of the entity.

While some of us--for whatever reason--seem to have been "born" with mediumistic abilities, I am convinced that everyone is more or less able to cultivate such talents. And I definitely encourage all those who seek to become fully developed New Age Magicians to put forth some effort toward establishing a link with the beyond.

DO NOT RUSH SPIRIT CONTACT

One cannot be dogmatic about which procedures work best for the encouragement of mediumship, but I can say with great certainty that the prime prerequisites are patience and practice.

All psychic development, if it is to be effective and lasting, must grow through a slow and gradual process. Do not attempt to rush your contact, and do not become discouraged if you do not become an overnight success as a medium.

BE SERIOUS

One of the primary essences of Indian Medicine is a strong belief in the partnership between the world of the physical and the world of the spiritual. If you begin your sitting out of a sense of silliness or levity, you are indicating your desire to fail at a most vital and serious project.

Some of you will probably achieve amazing results in a relatively short time. For others, the development of your powers may take weeks or months.

Take what comes to you, regardless of how small or irrelevant the manifestations may seem. Keep at it. Wait for better results. They will come if your perseverance and patience remain strong.

SET A REGULAR TIME

As much as possible, set a regular time for your development exercises. Don't overdo this by becoming a slave to the clock or by sitting too often.

Begin with ten-or-fifteen-minute sessions every other day, or twice a week. Daily sessions are all right, too.

Gradually increase your time allotment to half an hour a sitting. Don't go beyond that unless and until you reach the stage where manifestations occur regularly and may occasionally require longer periods.

The time of day most suitable for your early exercises and, for that matter, perhaps for all psychic training and experimentation, is the latter part of the evening -- when you are finished with the day's responsibilities, when your segment of the world has slowed down to a more serene pace.

The room in which you sit should be quiet, not too large, and sufficiently remote to assure privacy and safety from interruptions.

COMPLETE DARKNESS IS NOT NECESSARY

The lighting should be subdued. One bulb in a wall socket or a desk lamp is more than adequate--and even that should be shaded, possibly with a blue or purple scarf or some gauze of similar color.

Complete darkness is, of course, very desirable, as well; but sitting alone late at night in total darkness, attempting to make spirit contact, is often a bit unnerving for the novice medium. Let no one tell you that absolute darkness is essential to spirit manifestations.

EXPECTANCY

If you are conducting your experimentations alone--which is not the most desirable arrangement except for the first part of your training--place yourself in a comfortable chair and use the method that some mediums call "Expectancy."

Sit quietly.

Divest your thoughts of your immediate worldly concerns and attempt to keep your mind blank.

Place yourself in as receptive a mood as possible. Be alert, but don't expect anything particular to occur. Be patient and wait.

If there seem to be points of light darting about the room, understand that they could be caused by natural manifestations of eye strain.

If you hear the creaking of floor boards, recognize that the sound may be caused by changes in temperature rather than the appearance of an unseen spirit.

If your arms and legs become numb and cold, know that these sensations may be due to tiredness or rigidity, rather than the approach of the supernormal.

In other words, remain calm and don't become panicky or credulous. You will know well enough when the real thing comes.

Adjourn your expectancy sitting after ten or fifteen minutes. Repeat it a day later--or two or three days later--up to a total of a dozen times or more.

If genuine phenomena or raps do occur, don't be surprised and don't be frightened. Such things merely indicate that you are well on your way to mediumship and that you are gaining in psychic strength.

CRYSTAL GAZING

Use a crystal ball such as readily available through metaphysical bookstores or use a saucer full of ordinary tap or spring water. Or obtain a large piece of natural quartz crystal to serve as your window into other dimensions.

If you use a crystal or a glass ball, place it on

some dead-black material to eliminate glare, brilliant high lights, and reflections.

Make your mind a blank. Gaze--don't stare--steadily at the crystal, blinking as little as possible.

Don't permit yourself to become sleepy. Don't extend your steadfast gaze for more than five minutes at a time.

If your eyes begin to water, this may be taken as an indication that your time limit has been reached. You should then end your experimentation without delay.

Sooner or later in the course of your exercises, your crystal ball will cloud over and, when this passes, small figures may be seen moving about in the crystal itself. A varying panorama, not unlike miniature moving pictures may develop, and certain scenes will be acted out before your eyes.

These pictures and scenes--whether they are of familiar or strange locations--do not actually appear in the ball; they are merely projected into the crystal by your own subconscious mind.

If you are unable to see anything in the crystal, you can try to train your latent ability, or awaken and strengthen your visual memory, by first looking at a certain object in your own room and then trying to transpose it, mentally, into the crystal.

You might also close your eyes for a few minutes, think intensely of a person you know well, and try, with your eyes open, to see the picture of him or her in the crystal.

Not everyone is successful. Remember that, and don't be too disappointed if you are among those who lack this specific gift.

AUTOMATIC WRITING

Automatic writing is an aspect of communicating with the beyond that many men and women find preferable and more adaptable to their personal cosmologies.

Seat yourself comfortably at a table.

Place a piece of paper before you and hold a pen or pencil in your hand in the manner in which you usually write. Let its tip rest lightly on the paper.

Keep your wrist and arm loose, the wrist preferably in such a position that it does not touch the table at all.

Wait quietly and patiently. Close your eyes. Listen to flowing New Age music, such Steven Halpern's **Starborn Suite**.

Give in to the slightest impulse to move the pencil, keeping the paper smooth with your left hand.

It is not necessary--and in fact not even desirable--that you concentrate on your hand and what it is doing. If you do not wish to keep your eyes closed, you may even read a book while experimenting, just to keep your thoughts occupied.

See to it that no direct light shines on the paper. Shield it with a piece of cardboard or something similar.

Chances are, in the beginning, you will merely produce nervous squiggles without any meaning. But sooner or later, messages will come through.

It usually takes three or four sittings before the first intelligible results are achieved.

Don't prolong your sittings unduly, even after they do come. Be patient!

GATHERING A GROUP

Once you have begun to produce results in your experimentations, it is advisable to give up your solitary sittings and to work with one or more other persons. Not only does this considerably lessen the danger of fatigue or boredom, which may cause you to give up too early, but it is undeniable that two or three people, even during the period of preliminary training, can accomplish more than the single experimenter.

You must be certain, however, that you have picked like-minded individuals to participate in your sessions.

For obvious reasons, you would not be likely to ask any friends who are hardnosed skeptics, who would not be able to recognize a miracle should one occur in their presence.

At the other end of the pole, neither should you invite friends who are "true believers," who would see a sign of the supernatural in every click of the thermostat.

It would be most desirable to choose friends who have an interest in psychic development, a good deal of patience, and a rather well-established sense of balance.

Once you have found the right person or persons, you can greatly vary and enlarge your training experiments.

To begin with, go once again through the exercises described in this lesson. Once your fellow sitters have experienced these sessions, you can proceed to simple experiments in telepathy.

SENDER/RECEIVER

Appoint one of you to be the sender (or transmitter) and the other the receiver (or recipient). If a third person is in your group, let him or her be the observer and recorder, alternating these roles among you.

Let us say that you begin by assuming the role of the sender. Seat yourself at a table, brightly lighted by a lamp placed somewhat behind you and shining directly on a piece of paper in front of you.

Your face should be turned toward the place where the receiver is seated, some distance away, with his back to you.

On the piece of paper before you, draw a simple figure, such as a circle, a cross, a triangle, and so forth. For your early experiments it is wise to agree beforehand on four or five such basic designs to be transmitted.

After drawing the figure, focus your attention upon it. Concentrate on it for a minute.

Then, mentally, **will** the recipient to receive the impression that you are transmitting.

The recipient, in turn, tries to keep his or her mind a blank. If he is also seated at a table with a piece of paper before him and a pencil in his hand, he may sketch the figures that he has mentally received from you. Once the impression is received, the recipient should draw it without hesitation, announcing when he or she has done so.

After some practice, the results you will achieve will be rather amazing. You will find that the number of correct impressions received will figure out to be much higher than they would be if they were mere guesses. You will see them stretch far beyond the law of probability and chance.

THE CIRCLE

Once you have begun to work well together as a group it will be time to form your spirit "Circle."

Make it very clear that only those who are strongly intent upon establishing spirit communication should ever participate in your circle. Seances are never to be a matter of an evening's fun and entertainment.

While there are circles designed for research and scientific exploration, the more successful groups are those composed of men and women who care about one another and who are in harmonious spiritual accord. It has often been observed by mediums that sympathy, earnestness and purpose, harmony, and patience are prerequisites to success in establishing spirit contact.

How many people should belong to a Circle is a matter of individual preference. Two people may produce excellent results if their psychic talents have been sufficiently developed.

Through generations of experimentation, it has been set forward that four to six is a desirable number. Eight sitters seems to be the maximum number of seekers for the preservation of harmony and the elimination of discord.

Private Circles usually meet in the home of one of the sitters. The room set aside for the seance should be medium-sized, quiet, and so far as possible removed from street noises and other disturbances. It should be without a telephone, for nothing can be more disruptive than the sudden ringing of the telephone bell.

The room should be well-aired before the seance begins. It should be comfortably warm, but not overheated. Unless the banning of smoking causes one of the sitters distress, it should be discontinued during the actual session. The consumption of alcoholic beverages before and during the seance definitely should be banned.

Experience has shown that dry weather is best for the production of phenomena and that dampness or rain often hinder their occurrence. On the other hand, a sudden thunderstorm is very often conducive to the production of most unusual manifestations.

The best time for your Circle to meet is some time in the evening after dinner. You should choose a convenient hour when each of your sitters has had an opportunity to permit the day with its worries and responsibilities to have receded a bit into the background.

It is important that you sit regularly and always at the same time and place. Twice a week is the maximum number of seances for your Circle. A once a week meeting would be preferable

THE SEANCE

Each individual seance should last no longer than an hour. In the beginning of your sittings, it would be best to limit the sessions to about half an hour.

It should be understood from the very beginning that each person in your newly formed Circle must sit regularly and patiently for an absolute minimum of twelve seances. When you have completed the last session in the first cycle, permit the individuals to decide whether they care to continue studying and sitting with you.

Never restrain those members of the Circle who become dubious or bored. You should replace them with new sitters as soon as possible.

The first time your Circle meets, you would be wise to select a leader to be in charge of the proceedings, to ask questions as soon as a spirit communicator manifests, and to time the sittings. It must be agreed by all that each sitter will obey the orders of the leader and abide always by his or her arrangements.

It might also be a good idea to appoint a recording secretary, who will keep the minutes of each sitting and who will be certain that appropriate music will be provided.

The leader should assign seats around the seance table to members of the Circle, and once a seat has been assigned, it should be retained during the entire cycle of seances—unless developments unforeseen should make a change advisable.

The kind and intensity of light most appropriate for the development of spirit phenomena varies according to the psychic strength of the medium and the sitters. The best authorities of the subject consider it a kind of general rule that a bright white light is definitely detrimental to almost any kind of manifestation.

Seances by no means require complete darkness, but it is important that no direct light shines on the seance table.

Some Circles prefer sitting in darkness until the first unmistakable phenomenon occurs. From that point onward, a dim light is turned on.

A calm state of mind should be preserved by all sitters. It isn't necessary to be overly serious or to be gloomy. Just be open-minded and relaxed.

Try to convince everyone that intense concentration should not be attempted. Tension, excitement, fear, nervousness, can be as great a hindrance to the proceedings as arrogance, skepticism, and levity.

Wait patiently for what may happen. Don't be overly critical of what may manifest in those early stages. It is best in the beginning to accept what occurs, rather than to make immediate judgments and attempts to interpret.

Don't expect miracles, the levitation of one of the sitters, or dramatic psychokinetic manifestations. This is real life. Your seance has not been equipped with Hollywood-type special effects.

SPIRIT MANIFESTATIONS

When spirit manifestations begin, be cordial to the entities. Welcome them warmly; speak to them confidently and calmly.

Prepare questions that you wish to ask beforehand. When answers do come, do not flatly contradict them and do not break into laughter and declare that such things are impossible.

Later, when contact is firmly established, it will become possible to question the spirits and to ask them to more completely define matters.

All conversation with the spirit communicators should be carried on through the person chosen to direct the seance. Close adherence to this rule will not only prevent mix-ups and misunderstandings, but it will contribute greatly toward a more rapid progress in your Circle's development.

Don't set out to achieve any particular kind of manifestations, such as spirit materialization. Take whatever comes, and try to go on from there.

The messages which you will receive will vary greatly in value and content. Sometimes they will be absolutely startling, sometimes trifling, sometimes obviously transmitted in an attitude of teasing and gentle raillery.

The time that will elapse before the first phenomenon occurs and the transmission of veridical messages (messages that can be substantiated and proved) of sometimes great length and importance will vary greatly from session to session. On occasion, manifestations will start as soon as the lights are dimmed and the Circle closed. During other sittings, the participants may not be able to get beyond the simplest phenomena.

Almost certainly, though, results will get better and better and gain in importance from sitting to sitting. With the necessary patience and perseverance, some results will be absolutely certain to come through to you.

THE MEDIUM

Perhaps when your new spirit Circle assembles for your first meeting, you may be uncertain as to which of your number is the best one to serve as the medium. After the first timid manifestations begin to occur, it may be desirable to establish who among you is the actual medium.

This can be easily accomplished by asking each member, in turn, to leave the room. The moment the real medium has been eliminated from the circle, the phenomena will cease.

It is possible, of course, that more than one of your number is mediumistic.

In itself, the matter is unimportant. By the time that your Circle arrives at the more complex experiments, the question of who is the best medium will have been answered in a dozen different ways. The less powerful mediums--and all members of the Circle--will serve the principal medium as "batteries" enabling your Circle to produce increasingly impressive phenomena.

Remember always, that even the most modest of spirit gifts, including the simple ones of causing a table to tilt or a planchette to move, can be misapplied and abused. Each member of the Circle should seek to retain complete control over himself or herself and to practice at all times moderation and common sense.

Your basic repertoire and specialty as a Circle will depend upon your individual talents and tastes. You may use table tilting, Ouija boards, automatic writing, slate writing--whatever appeals most to you.

Many will favor trance speaking, thereby eliminating all mechanical intermediaries.

TRANCE

Trance is a completely natural and normal state. It comes about in psychically gifted persons in order to facilitate their communications with the world of spirit.

Since entranced people remember little or nothing of what takes place or of what they may say, it is important that the recorder of your Circle keeps careful written accounts of what has been uttered. Memory should not be relied upon.

Let us suppose that you are serving as the trance medium. Sit in the usual quiet seance room, holding hands with the person on either side of you. They, in turn, are holding hands with whomever is beside them, thus forming a circle around the table.

Sit for a moment of two listening to the restful music that should always be played during your sessions. Take a few deep breaths, holding them comfortably for a count of three.

Wait patiently.

Call out in a quiet voice, whatever letters, words, images, symbols, or impressions begin to come to you.

The recorder should be writing down all utterances for later examination.

In all likelihood, your state of trance will become deeper with each word or image that comes to you. The heightened interest of the members of the Circle will give you additional psychic strength.

MESSAGES

Messages will be delivered with increasing rapidity. Questions that your leader asks you to transmit to the spirit communicators will be answered immediately.

By the time that you and your Circle have reached the point where sittings for direct voice manifestations can be held with reasonable expectation, it will have been definitely decided who among your group is the most gifted medium.

When you hold your first direct-voice sitting, the seating arrangement should be different from the one which you have followed in all previous sessions.

The medium should occupy a chair set apart from the other sitters, who will now arrange themselves in a semi-circle in front of him or her. No hand-chain is formed, unless the link-up is preferred by the members.

The usual meditative background music should be played, and all lights should be extinguished. Sit quietly for a time or converse in low tones.

The medium should allow himself or herself to begin to enter the trance state. The Circle must remain patient and contemplative.

After a while, a whisper may be heard near the ear of one of the sitters. As soon as this occurs, the conversation and the music should stop. Expectant silence should prevail.

As in other seances, the sitters who find themselves addressed by the voices should attempt to identify the spirit speakers. This is an easy enough task if the voice is a familiar one, such as that of a departed friend or a family member. If one should hear the voice of a stranger, it is now permissible to insist upon positive identification.

In direct-voice sittings, by the way, the sitters are permitted to ask questions of the spirit entity directly, rather than through the intercession of the leader of the Circle.

Direct-voice seances are best held in complete darkness. If the Circle decides that some illumination is preferred, select a colored bulb (or cover the bulb with a colored scarf or a bit of gauze) that grants the most desired form of lighting.

PHYSICAL PHENOMENA

If there have been indications during your earlier sittings that one or the other of your Circle may be developing the ability to produce physical phenomena, the leader of your group must instruct all members to observe strict rules of seance etiquette. At no time, it must be emphasized, should the medium who is producing physical phenomena be touched during the trance state.

There are several tests which you may utilize to determine whether or not physical phenomena can manifest during one of your sittings.

During table tilting, for example, try lifting your hands from the top of the table without breaking the circuit. If the table continues to move and to tap out answers, you may proceed with seances especially called for the purpose of the producing of physical manifestations.

The same test would hold true for Ouija board and planchette seances. Lift your fingertips off the planchette. If it keeps moving, you have a clear sign that you may proceed with seances for physical manifestations.

For a physical seance, place several small objects, such as a bell, various musical instruments, small trinkets, and so forth, on the table. There should also be some carbon paper or paper blackened with soot, together with clean white sheets, for possible spirit fingerprints. You may also supply putty, clay, or wax for impressions.

The phenomena that may occur are manifold. There may be the levitation of the seance table, levitation of the medium, or one of the sitters. Light or heavy objects may be moved by unseen hands. The bell and musical instruments may be rung or played. They may even float about the room while invisible hands and mouths play them. By merely pointing at the seance table, the medium may produce raps.

Sittings for partial or complete materializations require the same sort of conditions which are necessary at seances seeking physical phenomena. All white light should be eliminated. The forming of a circle is important once again. Music is desirable.

Whatever happens, remain calm. Remember that no phenomenon is supernatural--only supernormal.

Frances' knowledge of the ancient wisdoms and her affinity for Egypt has earned her the designation of "Daughter of Isis."

CHAPTER SEVEN:
RECEIVE AWARENESS THROUGH VISION TEACHINGS

The Timeless Realm
Creative Energy
Living, Vibrational Truth
The Divine Fire

THOUGH the words "vision teaching" may seem selfexplanatory, the complete understanding of the entire concept of visions aids the seeker in attaining the desired result. Knowing what you will encounter once you embark on the quest of awareness helps the beginning of your journey.

For some, experience is the best teacher; but those, such as I, who have received vision teachings, feel that visions constitute the most thorough ways of gaining awareness.

Here, then, is a step-by-step description, so you might know the anatomy of a vision teaching.

When you are given a vision teaching, you are taken out of your body and lifted away from the physical dimensions of Earth. You feel more alive, more complete, and as if you are fully protected. You feel freer than you have ever felt before.

With your arms outstretched at your sides you soar vertically into space, higher and higher. The wind blows past you, tossing your hair. Your heart is filled with awe and love. Never before have you experienced such a wondrously beautiful feeling. Space is dark, but a multitude of colored lights sparkle around you. Stars, planets, nebulae, galaxies being born--the Milky Way moves soundlessly by.

You continue soaring higher and higher until you stop quite gently, as if standing in space. It is as though you hang suspended. There is a quietness in this stark realm that prepares you to open up to receive fully what you anticipate is forthcoming.

THE TIMELESS REALM

Here in this timeless realm you will receive visions, living diagrams, thought awareness. You can be shown the past and explore the previous lives that your soul has lived on Earth or in other dimensions of reality. You can understand more thoroughly your present situation, your mission to Earth. You can even receive the future. Sometimes diagrams appear that symbolically explain the great mysteries of existence--the questions humankind has asked since intelligent thought first formed in the more illuminated corners of the brain.

You have the ability to enter a dimension that operates on a higher vibration, where unconditional love, wisdom, and knowledge exist and can be given to you. With practice you can transcend to the space beyond the physical realm and lead a more meaningful and productive life.

Some teaching will be given to you in words, without an accompanying vision; yet the words create thoughts that permit the mind to imagine as if a diagram accompanied it.

When you permit yourself to enter an altered state of consciousness, you must want to receive awareness, to receive a vision teaching. You must desire to be taught, so that a greater understanding of many things may then be yours. This desire must be uppermost in your heart and mind.

You will be transported to a beautiful realm where a magnificent, colorful panorama of living diagrams, teaching of awareness, of past-life experience will be given to you. While you are in this realm, Unconditional love will permeate your entire being. It is in this dimension that angels, masters, and guides will visibly or invisibly interact with you, share with you, teach you all that you desire to know.

What you will see here cannot be contained. It must be shared, and it must not be permitted to stagnate. What you receive here and see here, *must* be shared with others.

In the giving, you will more fully understand what you have received; and you will be able to describe it and relay it more easily. You will also receive anew. You must give to receive, just as you must give away energy before you can receive the same energy afresh, anew. You must give love, wisdom, and knowledge before you will be able to receive them again anew.

When you receive such a vision, you will be totally happy for having had the contact occur, but you will also experience a sadness for your precious time that elapsed before such communication was made. Both of these emotions will be felt at the very same time. You will open your mouth to wail, to mourn, to laugh, and to shout for joy--all at the same time. This mixture of feelings accompanies contact with higher intelligences and vision teachings. There will remain no doubt that what you have witnessed has been from beyond, from the Source of all that is.

The receiving of a teaching vision comes when you are meditating, when your mind is quiet. Prayer is not meditation. Prayer is speaking, asking. Meditation is receiving, listening, waiting. If any mundane thought enters your mind, gently push it away. Never shove an intruding thought away from you. Instead, tell it that you will think of it later ...and gently, very gently, ease it from your mind.

With the eyes closed, most people see vague outlines of images or swirls. With practice the images will become clearer, focused, with colors coming in and going out. Soon the colors will remain and become vivid--then all will be clear.

CREATIVE ENERGY

Meditation is an art form wherein you receive the creative energy awaiting you. Soon you will become a part of the scene of the image, and you will experience it for a time.

Next, you will find yourself freely flying through space to a particular destination that has been selected by your higher self, your soul, or perhaps by your angelic guide, master, or teacher. When you reach this place, you will receive many awarenesses. You will feel the air move over your body, through your hair. You will feel freer than you have ever imagined. You will free yourself from the material world to which you have always been attached and step into the true reality of all that is.

Your vision teaching will come to you in a matter of minutes--ten at the very most, rarely more--though you may feel as though an hour has passed. This is a truth that appears universal; for in that domain, in the altered state of consciousness, there exists no sensation of time as we know it.

When you receive your vision teaching, a feeling of "knowing" will envelop you. You will feel that you have always known this awareness, and you will have an inner belief that what you have received is truth. You will feel it vibrate in your heart and in your stomach. as both will vibrate together, a heart and gut-level feeling. No one will be able to shake you from your belief in your teaching vision.

When you tell others of your teaching, you will be able to speak beyond what you were consciously aware of at the time you received the vision. This is due to your having not only absorbed the frequencies of higher awareness that accompanied the vision teaching, but also learned more than you were consciously aware of. You have thereby been elevated in your vibrational awareness. You will be able to comprehend more than you could have understood before the vision teaching was ever received.

By telling others you will become even more aware of the entire truth than when you first envisioned it, for you can now perceive it from many sides, thus gaining different perspectives. By giving you receive in greater abundance.

LIVING, VIBRATIONAL TRUTH

Vision teaching are parts of a living, vibrational truth that is composed of many facets of varying levels. Depending on your personal awareness, you will see the level of truth nearest your own understanding. As you grow in awareness, you will perceive deeper levels of that very same truth, as if you are ascending a beautiful, terraced landscape or a mountain that permits you to climb higher and higher. As you elevate your vibrations, rising in awareness, you will be able to achieve the highest level of consciousness; and thereby, one day. see all of the very same truth.

All truth teachings appear as separate visions to our understanding, awareness, and perception. Yet they are not separate at all. They are connected one to the other, as are the images on a great tapestry.

The more aware you become, the more your vision grows with you in depth and complexity until your awareness and higher vibration permits you to see it in its entirety. It is in this way that you discover the one truth, the Source of it all. It is in this way that you discover the Creator.

THE DIVINE FIRE

Stretching before you is something that appears to be a gigantic tapestry that has been woven of multicolored living lights, lights that are pulsating, throbbing with life. The lights have blended together, becoming one, yet they somehow remain separate.

The energy of the Divine Fire touches your inner self, and you are aware that you are becoming one with the great tapestry of life. In a marvelous moving, pulsating thrust of beautiful lights and living energy, your very essence feels a unity with all living things.

See before you an animal, any animal.
Become one with its level of awareness.
Become one with its essence.
Be that animal.
Be that level of energy expression.

See before you a bird, any bird.
Become one with its essence.
Become one with its level of awareness.
Be that bird.
Be that level of energy expression.

See before you a creature of the waters, any creature.
Become one with its essence.
Become one with its level of awareness.
Be that creature.
Be that level of energy expression.

See before you an insect, any insect, crawling or flying.
Become one with its essence.
Become one with its level of awareness.
Be that insect.
Be that level of energy expression.

See before you a plant, any flower, tree, grass, or shrub.
Become one with its essence.
Become one with its level of awareness.

Be that plant.
Be that level of energy expression.

Know now that you are one with the unity of all plant and animal essence. Know now that you forever bear responsibility to all things that walk on two legs or four, with all things that fly, with all things that crawl, with all things that grow in the soil, or sustain themselves in the waters.

See before you now a person, man or woman, that you find unattractive, perhaps even ugly.
Become one with this person's essence.
Become one with this person's awareness.
Be that person.
Be that level of energy expression.

See before you a child, boy or girl.
Become one with this child's essence.
Become one with this child's level of awareness.
Be that child.

See before you now a very old man or woman, perhaps someone confined to bed or to a wheelchair.
Become one with that old person's essence.
Become one with that old person's level of awareness.
Be that old person.
Be that level of energy expression.

Know now that it is never yours to judge another expression of humankind. Know now that you have a common brotherhood and sisterhood with all of humankind. Remember always that you must do unto your brothers and sisters as you would have them do to you. Remember always that the great error is to prevent in any way another's spiritual evolution.

At this eternal second in the energy of the eternal now, at this vibrational level of oneness with all living things, at this frequency of awareness of unity with the cosmos, the Divine Fire will permit you to receive a great teaching vision of something about which you need to know for your good and your gaining.

When you awaken, you will feel morally elevated; you will feel intellectually illuminated; you will know that your essence is immortal; you will no longer fear death; you will no longer experience guilt or a sense of sin; you will feel filled with great charm and personal magnetism;

you will feel better and healthier than ever before in your life; you will feel a great sense of unity with all living things.

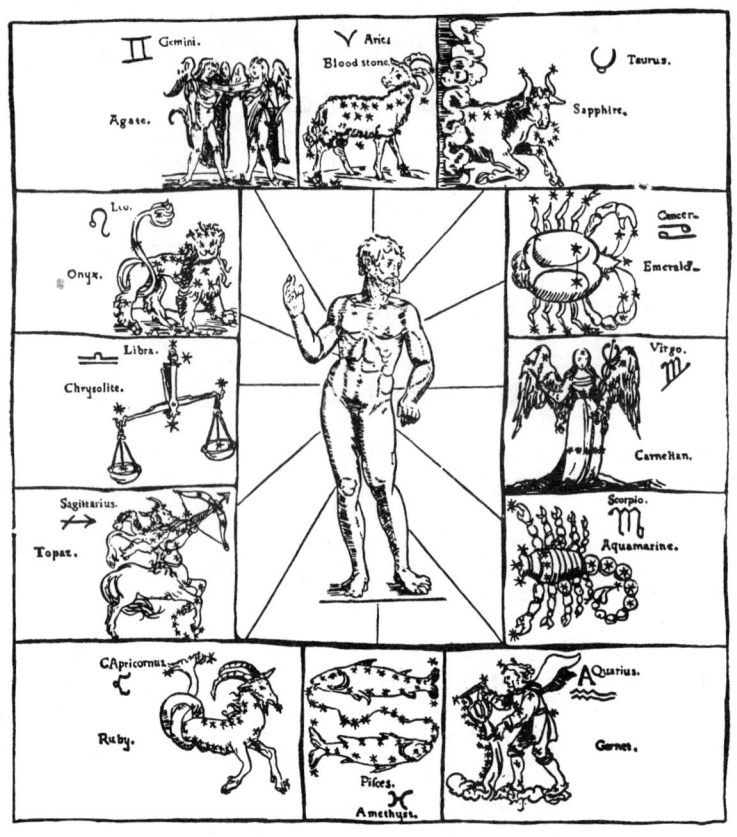

THE ZODIACAL STONES WITH THEIR SIGNS.

Old print illustrating the influence believed to be exerted on the different parts of the body by the respective zodiacal signs, and through their power by the stones associated with them. This belief often determined the administration of special precious-stone remedies by physicians of the seventeenth and earlier centuries.

CHAPTER EIGHT:
HEALING MIRACLES CAN BE YOURS

Healing Ability Lies Within You
Tap the Laws of the Universe
Our Mental, Physical, Spiritual Natures
Our Seven Energy Centers
Assume Control of Your Life
Rainbow Cloud Healing Technique

ALTHOUGH at no time have we declared ourselves to be "healers" in the sense that most people use that term, Brad and I have been privileged to serve as the channels for some remarkable healings.

There was the time when three women carried in their older sister, who had suffered from double vision and partial paralysis of her legs for over twelve years. After the woman had experienced a linkup with her Karmic Counterpart, she was not only able to walk straight and unassisted, she was able to dance the tarantella as her joyful sisters clapped and sang her accompaniment.

Once while a subject was deep in a trance, her arm began to move as if it were an independent entity. We frowned at one another in puzzlement as this occurred twice more during her awareness session. She awakened in tears of happiness and went straight to the telephone to call her doctor with the news that the arm that had been paralyzed for three years had now been fully restored.

A man who for several years had been unable to turn his neck because of fused vertebrae, awakened from his regression session laughing and swiveling his head freely from side to side.

TAP THE LAWS OF THE UNIVERSE

The universe is governed by laws that never fail, by forces that work without the consciousness of man. These energies, these powers, go beyond the present understanding of all humankind, but humankind does have the psychic ability to tap the powers governed by these laws. We have the ability to utilize the infinite currents that surround us and to absorb them into our own bodies.

It is this, the free will by which we can choose to tap into and absorb these energies, that divides us from other animals. But few of us utilize these forces to aid our lives. Few of us know how.

Our superconscious mind, more commonly called the soul, has eternal awareness, eternal consciousness, eternal wisdom, and eternal existence. We have within us the ability to tune into a mind more powerful than our own, whose boundaries are without limits, whose awareness is the universe. With access to all of this we need not want for anything. Throughout the ages our most revered leaders, master teachers, and prophets have told us of these universal powers that can make us perform miracles.

In the East Indian philosophy of yoga the human body is divided into seven zones. The yogic art of meditation, combined with body control, permits one to achieve with ease those feats which in the Western world would be considered impossible.

There are voluntary and involuntary muscles of the body; through yoga one learns to control both groups. But this physical control is not spirituality, for the serious student of yoga combines humankind's three basic natures into one and then establishes inner control over that one force.

OUR MENTAL, PHYSICAL, SPIRITUAL NATURES

There exists within each of us mental, physical, and spiritual natures. Learning to utilize these as one is the highest form of control over oneself. Everyone is a divine instrument capable of sending and receiving energy. Our sensory organs would best be described as receivers, for through them we receive sensory input, vibrations of various types. Our mind controls whether we will send or receive energy.

There also exists within us the ability to perceive beyond our five senses; this is known as extrasensory perception. All humans have this sixth sense, as do many lower animals. It has been conjectured that the sixth sense was perhaps far more developed in primitive humankind and that it contributed to the survival of the species. The sixth sense may have provided us with the ability to sense danger, giving us the necessary foreknowledge to aid escape.

OUR SEVEN ENERGY CENTERS

The seven zones of the body are governed by neurohormonal energy centers known as chakras. These seven chakra centers emanate from the spine. Opening these seven chakras, permitting them to operate at their fullest capacity, gives one total control over the mental, physical, and spiritual selves. There are various methods whereby we can learn to control our energy, directing it toward the chakra of our choice.

The seven chakras begin with the base of the spine, the sex glands. **The first of the energy centers controls the male and female generative organs of life.** Keep in mind the polarity of all energies that exist on the physical plane. The negative applications of the first energy center are anger, greed, and lust.

The second energy center is in the lower abdomen and it controls our body's lower portion, more specifically our legs and hips.

For a moment center your attention on this chakra in the lower abdomen. Close your eyes and feel the energy come into that area and emanate from it. You should be able to feel, even at this early time, a tingling vibration in your legs. The control of your lower body, its functioning and malfunctioning, comes from this chakra.

The third chakra is in the upper abdomen. This center controls the upper abdominal region, affecting all abdominal functions. This center, like the others, restores balance and harmony and cleanses all that it governs.

The fourth chakra is in the midchest. It is the very center of your nervous system. This is known as the heart chakra. This particular center is blocked in many individuals, for their mental and spiritual awareness does not encompass unconditional universal love. With others this chakra center is only partially open, having been opened by the love of one or more living things.

To cause this center to operate at its fullest capacity with balance and harmony, you must unconditionally, nonjudgmentally love all living things. An imbalance will cause various ills and malfunctions.

The fifth chakra is in the neck and it controls and balances the upper torso. It affects the communication of the individual. When this area is not open or is imbalanced, one can lose control. This chakra influences not only the arms and throat but sensitivity to pressures, currents of energies, temperatures, et cetera. Balancing and opening this energy center permits you further control of many of the glands and organs of your body.

The sixth chakra is what is commonly known as the "third eye," or individual consciousness.

Close your physical eyes and permit the magnetic waves to pulsate into this region between your eyebrows. Fix your attention on this center of energy. Not only will you balance your physical body, you will begin to contact your spiritual self.

Continued contact with your spiritual self will put you in contact with another very important part of your being, your soul. This is known as **the eye of wisdom.** Through this eye you will learn detachment from the physical world and grow in harmony with the cosmos. Through this chakra you will learn to become one with the supreme consciousness that flows throughout the universe. It is through this third eye that all that exists will be made known to you.

The last chakra is the seventh, the ultimate controller. When you learn to open, govern, and balance this chakra, the individuality that separates you from all of life will disappear. You will become one with the God force, one with the Source of all things, one with God. From this awareness you will attain eternal life, peace, wisdom, knowledge, and superconsciousness. It is this chakra that permits you **full** and total contact with your higher self, your soul. This state of oneness with the universe is known in East Indian philosophy as "Nirvana."

ASSUME CONTROL OF YOUR LIFE

Now that you are aware of the energies available to you, and know of the centers in your own body through which these forces can be channeled, you are ready to learn mastery of your mind, body, and spirit and to assume total control of your life.

First, be certain that all of your bodily needs have been acknowledged.

Wear comfortable, loose clothing. Place your body in a comfortable position, sitting straight-legged on a cushion with back against the wall or in lotus posture or lying down. Soft background music will aid you.

You may wish to have someone read this to you or make a tape of this method.

With eyes closed, begin breathing comfortably, deeply, slowly. Your breathing is getting slower now, slower now. Breathe for several minutes, clearing negative thoughts and all impurities from your body. Become sensitive to the coolness of the air that enters your nostrils and the warmness of the air that leaves. Concentrate on this sensation for at least a minute. Breathe very deeply.

Feel yourself leaving the lower existence for the higher existence.

Feel yourself leaving the darkness for the light.

Feel yourself leaving physical restrictions and rising to eternal immortality. You are leaving the unreal world for the true reality.

Repeat the following suggestions mentally and feel the sensations throughout your body: "I am relaxing my entire body. Beginning with my feet, legs, torso, arms, neck, face, and head, my entire body is relaxing, becoming more relaxed, more relaxed. My breathing is getting deeper now, deeper now, slower. I am completely relaxed.

"I am aware of the electromagnetic energies that surround me. I can feel these energies all around me. My entire body is bathed in the electromagnetic energies of the universe. An ocean of superconsciousness awaits me, coming nearer and nearer.

"With a deep breath I draw these energies into me, into me. I feel them come into my very being, nurturing me, nourishing every gland and cell of my body, filling me completely. Each breath that I take draws more of the universal energies into me, and I am full of the electromagnetic energies of the universe.

"My mind is gathering these energies together and focusing them at the very base of my spine. I feel all the energies collecting at the very base of my spine, humming, tingling, vibrating, and opening my first chakra. I feel my first chakra opening, opening, becoming positive and balanced.

"The energies are traveling up my spine and bursting into my second chakra, my abdominal chakra. I can feel my abdomen. My legs become balanced now, in harmony now with all that is positive.

"Now the universal magnetic energies are traveling up into my upper abdomen, my stomach region, and I can feel my third chakra open. I feel balance, harmony, and health fill my being as my third chakra opens and becomes energized.

"Universal magnetic energy is traveling further up my spine to my fourth chakra. It is entering the very center of my nervous system. It is entering my heart, and I can feel my heart open, open wider now, becoming balanced, more balanced, opening wider. Love, unconditional love, love for all that is, for all living things, for all of life, for God, for the universe, enters my being. My fourth chakra is open, and I feel the energy enveloping me, warming me; and I am filled with love as I've never experienced it--a deeper, more complete love.

"Now the magnetic energy is going farther up my spine to my fifth energy center, my fifth chakra, in my throat region. I can feel the energy entering, entering now, opening, opening now. The energy is filling my being, and I can feel it humming, vibrating, pulsating throughout my entire body. It is balancing me more completely and I will more fully be able to receive and give energies. It is balancing many of my glandular functions. My fifth energy center is open.

"The magnetic universal energies are rushing into the area between my brows, my third-eye region, my sixth chakra. I can feel the magnetic waves pulsating, tingling, throbbing. The energy feels wonderful. It feels so beautiful.

"A light before me is getting larger and larger now. The light is growing larger still and opening larger still, until it covers the entire vision of my third eye.

"I am aware of my spirit, and I feel my spirit within me moving. It is freer, becoming detached from the physical. It is leaving the physical, lesser, reality for the truer, spiritual, all encompassing reality. I feel one--one with all that is, one with the universe. I can now reach the higher consciousness that governs the entire universe. I desire to know all, for I seek the Source of all that is.

"The energy is now blossoming forth in my brain, like a thousand-petaled lotus blossom, opening up, petal by petal, one after the other.

"I feel the energies filling my mind completely, totally fully. I am in balance completely. My entire being is in balance, in harmony with all that is and with the universe. I am reaching for my higher self, my higher consciousness, my soul. I can feel its energies entering my being, I merge into it. My soul merges into me. We are one. We are one.

"From this day forth I vow forever to reflect my higher self, my soul, in all that I do. As I am merged into it and it is one with me, all things known by it are available to me. I am one with my higher self in the timeless realm. All love, wisdom, and knowledge can now be gathered here, and I desire to know many things. I thirst, and I shall be quenched. I hunger, and I shall be fulfilled!

RAINBOW CLOUD HEALING TECHNIQUE

Use any successful technique of your own to place yourself in a deep level of consciousness. Have someone read the following suggestions to you, or prerecord the suggestions and serve as your own guide via cassette tape.

You are so peaceful, so beautifully relaxed. You glance up into the blue, blue sky and pick the most attractive cloud that you can see. It is a rather small cloud, but it is exquisitely formed. It is a beautiful cloud with magnificent peaks.

You feel deeply at peace, looking upward at the cloud's fluffiness, its thick, rich fullness. It is soft and white, and it appears to be glowing...as it catches the rays of sunlight and shines with beautiful, prismatic colors.

As you watch the cloud, you wish to ride upon it, knowing that this special cloud would hold you safely in space. If you mounted the cloud, you would then be able to soar above the trees, the towns, the cities, Earth itself. You would be able to move into the heavens themselves. You could enjoy the beauty of the twinkling stars.

You could move so close to the stars. It would be as if you might reach out and touch them. As you move higher, the air would be fresh and pure. It would be a new world, a higher dimension. All would be so wonderful.

The cloud appears to be growing larger and larger ... larger still. And you notice that it appears to be floating toward you. You are happy inside. Perhaps someone up there heard your wish, for the cloud is lowering itself to you. You know that you will soon be able to climb aboard.

The cloud settles down right next to you. You know that you may now climb safely aboard.

You easily step over a full, puffy rim into the soft, fluffy center of the cloud. It is so comfortable on the cloud, so peaceful. And you can lie back as if you are lying down in an incredibly comfortable reclining chair.

Your cloud is so soft, so strong, so secure.

A ray of light shines forth from the heavens and touches your strong and fluffy cloud. It causes your cloud to glow softly. The radiance is different from any other light that you have ever seen. You can feel it as well as see it. It feels strangely wonderful, and it causes you to become very happy within yourself.

You know that you have felt this sensation before. Sometime before in your life it has touched your heart. It is the warmth of love . . . a beautiful, touching love. You feel so at peace, so happy, so loved. You begin to rise . . . floating slowly, gently, so very safely.

You know that you are protected by love from a higher power.

You begin to drift . . . drift and float . . . gently bobbing along like a cork in a pond. Drifting and floating. Drifting and floating. Drifting and floating. Higher and higher still.

As you drift . . . drift and float, you glance easily down toward the Earth. You can see the trees . . . the countryside . . . the cities and towns growing smaller and smaller until they look like tiny toys on a green blanket.

You are rising higher and higher, far above the ground. Smell the fresh winds as the air becomes fresher, cleaner, the higher you go. You breathe deeper and deeper, deeper and deeper, and you settle back comfortably on your cloud to rest and to enjoy the feelings of peace and of love all around you.

You are floating higher, higher, and higher. You are floating out of this time, out of this place, far out into the dimension form whence came that ray of beautiful light that made your cloud glow. You are going to that place in space where the warm, glowing light emanates.

There is an opening ahead, and it is coming closer and closer. You slip through the opening.

You can see now that it is not merely an opening, but a tunnel, a tunnel filled with myriad designs. And there is a light at the far, far end. See the light far ahead at the end of the tunnel.

The designs are sliding past you on all sides. Three-dimensional octagons are moving above you, beneath you, and on either side of you. Notice how perfectly these eight-sided objects are made.

Now you are speeding to the light at the end of the tunnel, barely noticing the designs. You are moving to that place in space where there is no time at all. You are coming swiftly to the end of the tunnel, and you slip easily through it into a strange and glorious place. This is a place that exists beyond time.

Now see before you a panorama of Earth from its beginning to your present date. Concentrate on the area of your body that is painful, diseased, or malfunctioning. See in your mind that particular body part about which you desire to know more.

Be aware that in that great expanse of time that lies before you your soul has led a particular lifetime that is directly affecting your body in the present. Whether it was a life experience that existed thousands of years ago, hundreds of years ago, a few generations back, or even if it was a forgotten event in your present lifetime, you have the ability to see before you the lifetime and the event that caused your present problem.

You have the ability to see that lifetime and to know all that occurred during that experience.

You will see all that transpired to cause the problem that so troubles you. See it. Know it. Understand it. Remember it. (Permit yourself approximately two minutes to contemplate your images and memories.)

Now you understand why you are suffering this problem. You see and know why the problem has come about. You are happy to have discovered where its roots lie.

And now, with the vibrations of this awareness, and with firm resolve to right all wrongs, to better existing circumstances, you are strengthened and know that you can be healed. You are wiser and stronger now, and you know deep within your heart that you can be released from the grasp of this event. You can be healed.

You glance down toward the east where a light, misty rain is falling, and you watch the sunlight sparkle through the tiny raindrops, which are transformed as if by magic into a myriad of sparkling diamonds. A beautiful rainbow appears, a rainbow that you know can heal you. The rainbow is formed from the colorful, prismatic glitter. See the stretching bands of lilac, rich lilac; rose, soft, beautiful rose; green, vibrant green; and sparkling, glowing gold before you. So beautiful. So near you.

You desire to pass through the healing rainbow upon your cloud and to feel the colors move all around and through you. You are going closer now, closer and closer. The rain has ceased, but the rainbow remains crisp and clear. You will start with the bottom color of gold and work up through all the colors to lilac.

You are passing to the **gold**--a glowing, sunny gold that touches your very being. You breathe much more deeply now, more freely now, as gold enters your body. You can see it all around you, glowing, warm and glowing. Gold is all around you and through you. Gold is going through you and you feel love enter your heart, mind, and body. You are now leaving gold and you enter into green.

Green--a very rich, living, healing green. Green as a fresh leaf. Feel and see the green all around you. Green, passing through you, healing your scars, wounds, pains, and troubles. A warmer loving sensation fills your being, and you leave green and pass into rose.

Rose--a delicate shade of rose, a pinkish shade of rose, so lovely, so beautiful. Rose all around you. Rose passing through you. You feel your heart being bathed in rose. Your heart is softer now, more pliable now, expanding and filling with an even richer, more beautiful love. You are leaving rose now and passing into velvety lilac.

Lilac--the most beautiful shade of lilac you've ever seen. Lilac passing through you. You feel yourself glow lilac, as your body is growing stronger and stronger, your love is growing deeper and deeper.

You are passing out of the lilac and leaving the rainbow. Before you, beaming down from the heavens is a rich, elegant shade of **violet**. Bright, glowing violet that is pulsating with life. Yes, the universal life-force is reaching down to you from the sky. It is touching your body.

You see **violet**, bright, glowing, pulsating all around you and you feel it within you. Violet is pulsating through your entire being. You can feel the lifeforce within you, and it feels so wonderful, so powerful, so beautiful, so good.

You feel yourself being filled with the most beautiful, perfect love that could possibly exist. Love, true love as it was always meant to be. Unconditional love. Non-judgmental love. Love without any conditions placed upon it. And this unconditional love fills your being. Love such as this exists throughout the universe. This love will sustain you in any crisis.

Now you see before you the Earth as a round ball. See the Earth beneath you suspended in space as a round blue ball. You are far above it, filled with love, unconditional love, perfect love.

Now imagine yourself as a kettle, complete with a spout, just as a tea kettle would be. The spout is where your heart is. Let your love pour out of your heart. Pour it over all lifeforms that exist, over all people, all animals, all life.

Pour forth your love over all living things and feel the violet ray of love energy touch you again and fill you once again with unconditional love. Feel it flow into you as you pour it out of you, pouring through you. As you pour, so you receive from above, giving and receiving unconditional love. You will always permit this love to flow into you and pour from you, to pour through you. You will be an instrument of this love vibration through the giving of this love. You feel strong, stronger than you've ever felt before. You feel healed within as well as without. You are clean, refreshed, balanced. You are renewed mentally, spiritually, and physically.

You will practice giving unconditional love from this day forth. You will give unconditional love to all living things when you awaken and before you go to sleep at night. You will give unconditional love throughout all your life and receive it afresh, anew. You feel whole, balanced, healed within and without.

You are beginning to descend. Your cloud is beginning to descend, going down, down, down. Back to Earth. You will remember all that you've seen, realized and experienced.

On the count of six all of your six senses will awaken and be made more perfect. **One**, your sense of taste . . . **Two**, your sense of smell . . . **Three**, your hearing . . . **Four**, your touch . . . **Five**, your sight . . . And **Six**, the most important of all, your intuition, your extrasensory perception, now awakens. Awake, refreshed, positive, healed, balanced, and filled with love, unconditional love for all.

These beads of Jadeite, Agate, Jasper, Serpentine and Rock Crystals from the Valley of Mexico were believed to have great healing powers by the local inhabitants.

CHAPTER NINE: THE WONDERFUL WIZARDRY OF COLORS

The first section is an analysis of what the various colors mean as applied to people's choices—runs the gamut from red to purple...19 colors...hues... shades

Mystical Color Beliefs
How to Breathe Color
Color Vibrations
Therapeutic Functions of Color
A Color Meditation to Balance Your Energies

MYSTICAL COLOR BELIEFS

ACCORDING to metaphysical scholar Keith Ayling:

"The ancients believed that each major color consisted of seven elements: a physical or material element, a vitality-giving power, a psychological element, a harmonizing quality, a healing power, an inspirational element and a spiritual or higher-consciousness element. To develop himself harmoniously a man was told to visualize the seven basic colors mentally every day to obtain the full benefit of their existence.

"Oriental occultists viewed the seven major colors as an ascending scale in the evolution of humanity. According to their calculations we have passed through the red, orange and yellow ray periods and are in the fourth or green epoch which will lead us to a higher period of growth and into the vibration of the beneficial blue rays from which we shall eventually pass into the ideal ethereal conditions of the indigo and violet rays. All these cosmic rays are said to emanate from the supreme White Light which is the source of inexhaustible energy, radiating as it does from the sun.

"Eastern mystics associate color vibrations with the **Chakras** of the human body.

The Violet **Chakra** is located at the top of the head, Indigo behind our forehead, the Blue within the throat where it regulates the thyroid gland, the Green near the heart and the Yellow, which controls the adrenal glands, the pancreas and liver, in the solar plexus.

"The Orange **Chakra** is centered in the spleen and the red at the base of the spine. Each **Chakra** is said to absorb a special current of vital energy through its particular color ray. The Orange **Chakra** for instance draws in **prana** or life energy from the sunlight and distributes it to all parts of the body. Directly associated with air intake. the activity of this **Chakra** is determined by the rhythm of our breathing.

"Deep breathing is of incalculable value because it enables the body to draw in a considerable supply of physical **prana** which is not possible with shallow breathing."

HOW TO BREATHE COLOR

As it is generally believed in mystical philosophies, the air we breathe contains a vital force, called **prana**. By filling our lungs and holding the breath for a few seconds, we can extract this vital force to benefit our physical and spiritual well-being. To obtain the maximum physical and spiritual benefits, breathing should be rhythmic--inhalation and exhalation being of similar duration with a short pause between the two processes. To begin, inhale for a count of 12 pulse beats, hold the breath for six, and exhale for another 12 beats. With practice, you may feel like increasing the duration of each operation, but don't strain.

Yogis recommend the practice of the "complete breath," which brings our entire respiratory apparatus into use. According to Keith Ayling, it is done in the following way:

Standing erect, or sitting with spine straight, steadily inhale through the nostrils, first inflating the lower section of the lungs, thus allowing them to push out the lower part of the diaphragm. Then, fill the middle part of the lungs to push out the lower ribs and the breast bone, and finally fill the upper area of the lungs to contract the lower part of the abdomen.

Retain this breath for six pulse beats--no more to start--and exhale slowly, lifting your abdomen as the air goes out of the lungs. Even if you are not breathing color, this method of breathing will give you an appreciable lift.

"The secret of color breathing is to keep in mind the idea that you are inhaling the color you believe you need to restore your health," said Ayling. "As you inhale the yogic complete breath, you should visualize the air you are breathing as being tinted with the color you desire.

"In your mind's eye, follow the course of your tinted breath through your body. During the short retention period, imagine it is flooding the area you wish to improve.

"You can begin by using the white light, considered to be the most powerful healer of all, representing as it does the light of the sun."

COLOR VIBRATIONS

It is also of vital importance to concentrate on the area of your body that requires healing. Some color therapists advocate telling the affected part to heal itself. Speaking aloud can help; words have vibrations.

Some researchers have suggested that while inhaling you say the following silently to yourself:

"I project the white light (or whatever color you are using) through my body to aid me in restoring health, vitality, and youthful beauty to my entire system."

If you wish, you can repeat it aloud between the deep breaths and thus benefit from the verbal vibrations. Doing this for three minutes in the morning and three in the afternoon usually produces a surprising effect. But again, don't overdo it.

THERAPEUTIC FUNCTIONS OF COLOR

Here are some therapeutic functions of the various colors as shared by Ayling:

To attain a youthful figure and eliminate wrinkles and flabby flesh, concentrate on a **rose-pink**, the color of youth and restoration.

Blue is considered to be the universal pain killer. When inhaling this soothing color, you should imagine that it is flowing through your tissues, removing the poisons and revitalizing your body. Blue inhalation can be used to alleviate sore throat, fever, and eye troubles. It is also recommended for convalescence.

If you've been sick, use both **blue and green** in harmony with appropriate affirmations. Should you feel lonely, depressed, or tired as is often the case after illness, you can visualize inhaling these two gentle, soothing colors, always remembering to fortify them with affirmations.

For lack of bodily energy, and for help on those days when you don't feel like doing anything, think **orange**--the vitality ray. For some, this may be the most important and effective color inhalation.

To obtain general good health and vitality, you can practice inhaling **red, rose,** and **orange**.

Red is said to be the easiest color to visualize. It also counteracts anemia.

Green is sedative and relaxing. It overcomes the stress of daily living and induces a sense of peace.

Yellow stimulates the brain, the spinal cord, and the solar plexus.

Violet is said to help headaches and neuralgia. It also stimulates the pineal gland.

The **white light** is credited with having the power of universal regeneration. It can be visualized as a combination of all other rays.

Color breathing can play a vitally important role in our daily lives.

If you are **habitually depressed** and gloomy, you should try inhaling **all the rays in turn**, the first in the morning after waking. Do the same for five minutes before going to sleep.

Watch carefully for the results and gradually eliminate the inhalation of one ray each day, in order to discover the most beneficial. In the morning, always end with deep inhalations of the **yellow ray**. Once you have discovered the ray which seems most beneficial for you, continue to inhale it, using an appropriate affirmation to help to change your outlook on life.

If you need more **money**, breathe deep, **rich green** to help banish your poverty vibrations--for that's what ails you. The green vibrations will attract what you need and want--money, friends, love, material comforts.

By affirming the benefits you are acquiring as you inhale the green ray, your life will change. Your consciousness will become rich and your personality magnetic. The ancients hailed green as the blessing of plenty.

The following are some general rules to help you obtain the fullest benefits from color breathing:

Banish from your mind all thoughts of illness, trouble, fear, and limitation. In particular, don't think of what ails you by name. Think of your mind as the **sun** of your body. Think strong, creative, and good thoughts about yourself.

See yourself in the state of health you desire. Use your own affirmation--and believe in it. Realize that you will definitely receive your supply of the cosmic healing force.

A COLOR MEDITATION TO BALANCE YOUR ENERGIES

Visualize that at your feet lies a blanket the color of **ROSE.** The color of rose stimulates natural body warmth and induces sleep. It also provides one with a sense of well-being and a great feeling of being loved.

Now you see that blanket is really a kind of auric cover, a rose-colored auric cover. Imagine that you are willing the blanket-like aura of rose to move slowly up your body. Feel it moving over your feet, relaxing them; over your legs, relaxing them; over your stomach, easing all tensions; moving over your chest, your arms, your neck.

Now, as you make a hood of the rose-colored auric cover, imagine that the color of rose permeates your psyche and does its part in activating your ability to balance all your body's energy levels. Once you have done this. visualize yourself bringing the rosecolored aura over your head.

The color **GREEN** serves as a disinfectant, a cleanser. It also influences the proper building of muscle and tissue.

Imagine that you are pulling a green, blanket-like aura over your body. Feel it moving over your feet, cleansing them; feel it moving over your legs, healing them of all pains. Feel it moving over your stomach, ridding it of all pains. Feel it moving over your chest, your arms, your neck--cleansing them, healing them.

As you make a hood of the green-colored auric cover, imagine that the color of green permeates your psyche and does its part in activating your ability to regenerate of parts of your physical body. Once you have done this, visualize yourself bringing the green-colored aura over your head.

GOLD has been recognized as a great strengthener of the nervous system. It also aids digestion and helps you to become calm.

Visualize now that you are pulling a soft, beautiful golden aura slowly over your body. Feel it moving over your feet, calming you. Feel it moving over your legs, relaxing them. Feel it moving over your stomach, soothing any nervous condition. Feel it moving over your chest, your arms, your neck.

As you make a comfortable hood of the golden aura, imagine that the color of gold permeates your psyche and strengthens your nervous system so that your body-brain network will serve you to better become a New Age Magician. Once you have done this, visualize yourself bringing the GOLD-colored aura over your head.

Researchers have discovered that **RED-ORANGE** strengthens and cleanses the lungs. In our modern society with its problems of pollution, our lungs become fouled whether we smoke cigarettes or not. Yogis and other masters have long known that effective meditation, effective altered states of consciousness, can best be achieved through proper techniques of breathing through clean lungs.

Visualize before you a red-orange cloud of pure oxygen. Take a comfortably deep breath and visualize some of that red-orange cloud moving into your lungs. Imagine it travelling through your lungs, cleaning them, purifying them, bearing away particles of impurities.

Now, visualize yourself **exhaling** that red-orange cloud of oxygen from your lungs. See how soiled with impurities it is. See how darkly colored it is.

Take another comfortably deep breath. See again the red-orange cloud of pure, clean oxygen moving into your lungs. See the red-orange cloud purifying your lungs of the negative effects of exhaust fumes, smoke, industrial gases. Exhale the impurities, then breathe again of the purifying, cleansing red-orange cloud.

YELLOW-ORANGE will aid oxygen in moving into every organ and gland of your body, purifying them, cleansing them. Imagine before you now a yellow-orange cloud of pure oxygen.

Take a comfortably deep breath and inhale that cleansing, purifying yellow-orange cloud into your lungs. Feel the yellow-orange cloud moving through your body. Feel it cleansing and purifying every organ. Feel it cleansing and purifying every gland. If you have **any** area of weakness or disease **anywhere** in your body, feel the yellow-orange energy bathing it in cleansing, healing vibrations.

As you exhale all impurities and inhale again the pure, clean yellow-orange cloud of oxygen, visualize the cleansing and healing process throughout your body. As you exhale and inhale, see your body becoming pure and clean. See now that the cloud that you exhale is as clean and as pure as that which is being inhaled. You have cleansed and purified your lungs. You have cleansed, purified, and healed all of your body and all of its organs.

The color of **VIOLET** serves as an excellent muscle relaxant. Violet is a tranquilizer. It is a color of the highest vibration.

Imagine that you are pulling a violet, blanket-like aura over your body. Feel it moving over your feet, relaxing them. Feel it moving over your legs, relaxing them, soothing them. Feel it moving over your stomach, removing all tensions. Feel it moving over your chest, your arms, your neck -- tranquilizing them, relaxing them.

Now, as you fashion a hood of violet-colored auric cover, imagine that the same color of violet permeates your psyche and does its part in activating your ability to use true magic. Feel the color violet attuning your psyche to the highest vibration. Feel the color violet connecting your psyche to the God-Energy. Once you have done this, visualize yourself bringing the violet-colored aura over your head.

BLUE is the color of psychic ability, the color which increases visionary potential.

Visualize a blue blanket-like aura beginning to move over your body. Feel it moving over your feet, relaxing them. Feel it moving over your legs, soothing them. Feel it moving over your stomach, your chest, your arms, you neck -- soothing them, relaxing them.

As you make a hood of the blue-colored auric cover, imagine that the color of blue permeates your psyche and does its part in activating your ability to meet the spiritual guide who can most completely assist you in achieving the most important acts of Magic. Once you have done this, visualize yourself bringing the blue-colored aura over your head.

You are now lying or sitting there totally wrapped in your blue-colored auric cover. You are very secure, very comfortable, very relaxed. Your mind is very receptive, very aware. You feel attuned with a Higher Consciousness. You feel as though your awareness has been expanded. You know that all of your energies of mind, spirit, and body have been balanced.

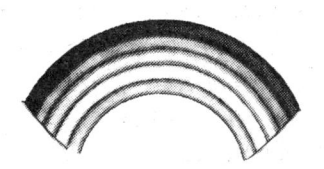

CHAPTER TEN:
CHARMS, AMULETS AND RINGS

Creating Charms with Candles
Using a Wax Image to Charm
The Ancient Lucky Seven Love Ritual
A Ritual for Summoning a Spirit of the Dead
The Love Ritual of the Seven Knots
A Tree Charm to Gain Strength
The Incredible Magic in Stones and Gems:
How to Use Them in Amulets and Rings

CASTING CHARMS WITH CANDLES

LOVE

SINCE the Middle Ages it has been believed that a candle formed in the image of a witch and burned with the proper incantation can bring love to the magician. Such witch-candles are easily available, especially around Halloween, and certain love-seekers might see fit to buy up a healthy supply from their local variety stores. According to tradition, a redcolored witch candle brings about the best results.

First, goes the charm, anoint the witch-candle with perfume to signify femininity. Once this has been done, allow the candle to burn for ten minutes and offer this short invocation: "O loving spirits of Diana, let this offering to you help bring my lover ---(name) to me for now and forevermore."

The invocation should be made at sunset. It should be said once over the flame of the witch-candle, then the candle should be extinguished and the invocation repeated over the smoking wick. The spell should be repeated on consecutive sunsets until the candle has been consumed.

DISPELL EVIL

A black candle formed in the shape of a skull (also readily available around Halloween) has long been utilized in ceremonial magic to dispell curses.

The skull-candle should be burned at midnight and a proclamation, which has been formally written on paper, is to be read above the flame: "In the name of the Mystic Skull, I ---(the magician's name) do hereby remove any curse that has been set against me."

The candle must be anointed with oil and must be burned for exactly one-half hour, beginning precisely at midnight.

The process should be repeated on the following night, and this time, the proclamation should be burned near the end of the half-hour period. The ashes of the paper should be left before the sputtering candle for the remaining few minutes, then the flame should be snuffed.

POWER AND SUCCESS

Power and success may be gained through the ritual burning of a candle formed to the shape of a mummy's sarcophagus. One first anoints the candle with oil and sets before it an incense offering of sandalwood or myrrh. The candle is lighted to the following incantation:

"The Soul of the Gods is in Unas, the Spirit-Souls are with Unas and the offerings made unto him are more than those made unto the Gods. Unas is the Great Power, the Power of Powers, and this offering will bring his powers unto ---(the magician's name), who does it, and success shall be mine."

REMOVING A SPELL

If one should feel that he has become the unwelcome recipient of a candle spell, he may reverse its effect through an ancient Medieval candle burning ceremony.

The alerted victim should, for five nights in a row, light two large, black candles just as the sun is phasing into dusk. As the candles burn, the supplicant should recite this invocation:

"Beezlebub and all evil spirits, in the name of Astaroth and the Light and the Dark and the Gods of the Netherworld, remove thy curse and thy sting from the heart of ---(the supplicant's name) and whosoever shall be casting a curse against me, let he or she suffer his own curse. Let these candles be his candles, this burning be his burning, this curse be his curse. Let the pain that he has caused me fall upon himself!"

The two candles must be allowed to be completely consumed each night.

THE ANCIENT LUCKY SEVEN RITUAL

This ritual goes back to the early Middle Ages and has become a legendary magical method of gaining a desired lover's affection. It requires a cauldron of the first rain water in April (distilled water will do).

As the water boils, the following ingredients are to be collected and stirred into the Cupid's brew: seven hairs from a blood snake, seven feathers from an owl, seven scales from a snake, a hair from the object of love and a bit of his nail paring.

When all the ingredients have been incorporated into the cauldron, allow the magical "stew" to boil briskly for seven minutes. At the end of this time, you must permit the brew to cool before you sprinkle it upon your intended. It should be your desire merely to warm your lover up a bit, not to scald him!

(**Author's note:** All of the above ingredients seem relatively easy to obtain with the exception of the "seven hairs from a blood snake." After burrowing through several reference works, I found that "blood worm" was a slang term for sausage and bologna. It may be that "blood snake" was also a colloquialism for sausage prepared in the gut and/or hide of a pig. In that case, a "blood snake" could, perhaps, yield seven hairs.)

THE LOVE RITUAL OF THE SEVEN KNOTS

The expression "tying the knot" when one speaks of the marriage vows seems to have almost universal meaning. African friends have told me of similar "knot-tying" love spells in their own tribes. Somehow it seems the most natural kind of symbolism to visualize the binding of one's self to the object of one's secret love while the fingers weave the knots and the lips chant a soulful litany.

Here is how the ancient love spell of the seven knots was woven:

The magician would take a length of cord or ribbon which would sustain seven knots strung out at a distance of about an inch from one another. According to the ritual, the first knot was to be tied in the middle of the cord with these words:

"This First Knot ties up and encircles the physical being of ---(name of the loved one) so that he remains bound to me from this moment. The very utmost strength of my love and my will is within the circle and binds --- to me."

At about the distance of one inch, the conjurer would form the second knot to the right of the first.

"With the Second Knot, I seize the will of --- with my own, which is like the strength of steel. My love --- will not say anything or do anything that will not be in fullest accord with my wishes."

The third knot was tied to the left of the first knot.

"With the Third Knot I now encircle ---'s love and clasp it firmly to mine. He will not be able to break away from me even though he might intend it. He will not be able to loosen my spell."

The fourth knot was to be placed to the right.

"The thoughts of my love will be completely held to my own. My love --- will never be able to remove the image of my person from his mind. He will always execute my just desires as forcibly as I execute them now by the forces of our beautiful Diana and of the ardent prayer which I dedicate to all good spirits so that the Holy Light will ever be my counsel and keep me from bad intentions."

The fifth knot was done to the left.

"The Fifth Knot imprisons the heart of ---, and he will not be able to, nor will he try to, fall in love with any other woman. His heart will be devoted only to my happiness and my love."

The sixth knot was bound on the right.

The Sixth Knot binds ---'s words, thoughts, doings, and desires to me alone from this day forward and forever more."

The last knot, the seventh, was secured to the left and with the speaking of the following words the spell neared completion.

"The Seventh Knot makes ---'s love completely mine, and with this knot I completely enclose him with the magic circle of this magic ribbon. With this shall I surround his heart; with this shall I love his heart; with this shall I love his entire physical being and will that his physical being shall be mixed with my own physical person. With the tying of the Seventh Knot, we shall stand together forever, and nothing, nor any one, will be able to tear us asunder or destroy our happiness."

The incantation completed, the maker of the ritual would then bind the two ends of the cord together and wear it in the manner of a garter upon her left arm above the elbow. The "seven-knot-love-garter" was to be worn to bed for seven alternate nights. Upon the fourteenth day, the charm was either to be burned in offering to Diana or to be hidden in a secret place.

A TREE-CHARM TO GAIN STRENGTH

Trees, an occultist explained to me, are a "...good source of radiant vitality on a very low-frequency scale" and may be drawn upon for "relief, and even cure, of backache conditions."

The prospective charm-maker is advised to select a suitable tree, "strong, upright, free from distortions... and of good size." Ash, spruce, and birch (definitely not yew) are recommended. For best results, the tree should be situated as far away from "human contamination" as possible.

Once a proper tree has been selected, the magician "makes friends" with it by "touching it, talking to it, and thinking into it." The tree should be circled nine times while the magi touches it gently with his fingertips or with the tip of his staff.

Upon the completion of the encirclement, take a final position to the North, lean back against the tree "firmly as if in the arms of a friend," and reach your hands behind you so that they might touch the bark of the tree. In this position, chant audibly:

> O Tree;
> Strong Tree; King Tree:
> Take thou this weakness of my back.
> Give me strength instead.
> That I may be as upright as thyself
> Between the Heavens **(look up)**
> And the Earth beneath **(look down)**
> Secure from storm
> And blessed in every branch.
> **May this be so!**

Repeat the incantation until you begin to feel a rapport with the tree. Once this has been sensed, relax, lean back against the tree, and allow it to work on your back for ten minutes.

"After a little while," the occultist said, "there should be a 'pulling out' feeling in the back which varies with individuals. When it is felt that the treatment is over, break contact gently, thank the Nature Spirits for their help, 'pay' the tree by sticking a pin into the bark, and take a small piece of the bark for a 'pocket-link' to carry with you."

THE INCREDIBLE MAGIC IN STONES AND GEMS

The Rev. Richard De A'Morelli has shared his arcane knowledge of the hidden magic in stones and gems and how best to use them in amulets and rings.

"Amulets can bestow complete control of the material plane and destiny; perhaps this explains why this knowledge has been forbidden for the uninitiated down through the centuries," Rev. De A'Morelli explained. "Magical gems are not and can not be intended for use by the careless or foolish at heart.

"Perhaps the most popular amulets are the 12 birthstones. These semi-precious gems, mounted in rings and pendants, are usually sold to astrology buffs, but also have widespread appeal. Because most people are familiar with these stones, the magic powers of each will be considered here."

Diamond--This precious gem is astrologically associated with the sign of Aries. A diamond amulet traditionally symbolizes enduring love and happiness in a marriage. Given as a gift, the gem strengthens emotional bonds and promotes loyalty.

A diamond pendant may be worn to obtain honor and friendship. Mounted in a ring, the amulet insures lasting marriage and financial success.

Emerald--Traditionally associated with the astrological sign Taurus, this precious green gem has several unique properties.

An emerald pendant affords women protection against rape and defilement. Mounted in a ring, the stone promotes domestic stability and fortune.

According to the legend, this amulet may be used to combat epilepsy, depression and insanity.

Agate--This stone may appear as stripped or clouded quartz, and is astrologically associated with the sign Gemini.

An agate amulet worn as a pendant promotes good health and fertility.

An agate ring bestows wealth and honor; also, it can be used to obtain favors from people in high positions. Legend has it that any person who gazes upon this charm will be compelled to speak the truth and cannot maintain secrecy.

Ruby--This popular birthstone, which is associated

with the astrological sign Cancer, reputedly promotes mental health and tranquility.

A ruby pendant combats depression and enables the wearer to overcome sorrow. A ruby amulet worn as a ring bestows knowledge, health and wealth.

This stone should never be given as a gift, as it will result in discord and broken relationships.

Sardonyx--The birthstone of Leo people. this gem is a popular remedy for impotence. Ancient occultists believed that a sardonyx amulet could be worn to alleviate this affliction in less than a week.

Mounted in a ring, sardonyx has no power; however, worn as a pendant, the stone combats sterility. Given as a gift, the sardonyx amulet guarantees the recipient's fidelity.

Sapphire--This deep blue corundum is astrologically associated with the sign Virgo.

A sapphire pendant is a reputed cure for fever, seizures, and delusions. Mounted in a ring, the gem bestows wisdom and compassion.

When danger is imminent, this amulet reportedly takes on a chalky appearance, which remains until the hazard has subsided.

Opal--This semi-precious gem is associated with the astrological sign Libra.

Worn as a ring, this amulet reputedly alleviates indigestion and other stomach disorders. Also, it instills tranquility and joy. An opal pendant is worn to attract happiness in love, fortune and favorable judgment in court.

The opal amulet takes on a dull gray appearance when minor illness is forthcoming. A sickly yellow hue presages injury by accident.

Topaz--This semi-precious gem is the birthstone of Scorpio people.

Some medieval occultists insisted that a topaz amulet promoted psychic sensitivity and facilitated control of destiny.

A topaz pendant reputedly bestows honor, happiness and inner peace in addition to the above benefits. Mounted in a ring, the gem insures promotion and financial success.

Turquoise--This gem, which is the birthstone of Sagittarians, has been worn in amulets since the earliest times. American Indians considered the stone sacred, and medieval sorcerers used it in various magic rituals.

Modern authorities claim that a turquoise amulet is an effective deterrent against illness and injury.

Worn as a pendant, the stone also protects its bearer from a violent death. A turquoise ring may be worn to rekindle old love affairs and obtain emotional gratification.

Garnet--This semi-precious gem is the birthstone of Capricorn people.

The stone was used extensively by early Egyptians and Phoenicians. It reputedly healed snake bite and food poisoning by absorbing alien chemicals in the blood through the skin.

A garnet pendant is usually worn to arouse the passionate love of the opposite sex and to obtain physical gratification. A garnet ring reputedly combats fear and pessimism.

Argument and eventual separation of two lovers results when garnet is given as a gift.

Amethyst--This gem, a purple variety of quartz, is traditionally considered to be the Aquarian birthstone.

An amethyst ring is usually worn for protection against sorcery and the Evil Eye. An amethyst pendant prevents depression and supposedly bestows spiritual visions.

Bloodstone--Also known as heliotrope, this variety of quartz is the Piscean birthstone.

Worn as a pendant, it prevents miscarriage and other illness during pregnancy. Mounted in a ring, the amulet reportedly promotes affluency and creativity.

Worn to bed, bloodstone may bestow pleasant dreams and clear visions of the future.

In addition to the twelve birthstones described above, there are five other gems of magical significance which warrant consideration. These are as follows:

Amber--This gem, which has been used for magic purposes from time immemorial, is primarily a health aid.

An amber pendant reportedly cures diseases of the blood, poor circulation and prevents heart attack. Mounted in a ring, this stone combats malfunction of the kidney and protects the wearer against heat stroke and suffocation.

Beryl--This opaque stone usually comes in yellow, pink, green or white. Worn as a pendant, it promotes happy marriage and honesty. Given as a gift, it is a popular deterrent to unfaithfulness.

A beryl ring is frequently worn to insure good health during pregnancy.

Carnelian--This reddish quartz gem was highly popular with Old World occultists. Early Chaldeans gave the stone to enemies and thereby rendered them harmless.

According to legend, the person who wore this stone, either as a ring or pendant, became sickly and listless, thus incapable of competition.

Coral--This stone occurs in a variety of colors and is allegedly invaluable to careless people.

This amulet takes on a chalky white appearance when in close proximity with sick people. A coral ring or pendant may also be worn to promote health and wisdom.

Jade--Throughout history, man has used this gem as a deterrent to sorcery and demonic possession. Jade is therefore considered to be one of the most potent protective devices known to mankind.

Modern occultists claim that a jade pendant may be worn to achieve the above effects, and that a ring combats tragedy and depression.

Jet--Perhaps one of the most powerful amulets known, this lustrous black gem holds an important place in the legends of various cultures. In ancient Greece, occultists believed that it was a sacred substance, and in Assyria it was considered to be the gods' favorite jewel.

Medieval legend credits the jet amulet with supernatural powers. The person wearing this stone supposedly attains complete control of the natural elements--fire, air, earth and water. To accommodate this purpose, a jet pendant is usually worn.

CRESCENT OF ROCK CRYSTAL FROM VALLEY OF
MEXICO, TROCADÉRO MUSEUM.

CHAPTER ELEVEN:
CHANTS AND CEREMONIES

Rites of Preparation
The Magician's Cloak
Oil for Annointing
The Ceremony
How to Make a Curse-Removing Puppet
Do-It-Yourself Exorcism
A Crusader's Sword to Ward Off Evil
Ritual to Know All things
The Formula of Ceremonial Magic

A VISIT FROM SEKHMET

ON December 2, 1974, I interacted with an external entity in some in-between universe in a dramatic experience that I shall never forget. It would appear that the Egyptian goddess Sekhmet reached across Time and Space to cement a bond that may have been first established centuries ago.

I had been standing speaking to my older son when I suddenly felt dizzy. I could feel myself losing consciousness, so I turned to walk to my bedroom. I began to fall somewhere mid-doorway, but I landed face down in the sand of some mysterious far arena.

Frighteningly, I could hear crowds of people shouting for my death. "He's down! Kill him! We've got him now!"

I felt as though I were a downed gladiator, but I obviously had my supporters, for I could also make out some people screaming at me to get up. "You can do it!" they yelled. "Get up and live. Put your legs under you and stand up!"

I moved my head sideways in the dirt and the sand and saw that I lay in what appeared to be an ancient arena for trial by combat. In spite of the raucous shouts of condemnation and the supportive cheers of encouragement, I could see no more.

Then a figure moved from the shadows, a figure nearly as dark as the shaded area from whence it came. Its body was unmistakably that of a woman, but her face was that of a lioness.

She stood before me, reached down a helping hand, and pulled me erect. As she opened her mouth to speak, great bolts of electricity shook and revived my body. Although I could not clearly distinguish the words which she spoke to me, I received images of concepts, both minute and major, and the faces of men and women I knew I would soon meet in physical reality.

When I regained full consciousness, I lay on my bed, still pulsating from what seemed to be those same great bolts of energy. Somewhere between this world and the archetypal world, I had been brought to an awareness and an energy by the goddess Sekhmet

Sekhmet is one of the most ancient of deities, who came into Egypt in a time unrecorded from a place that is unknown. She is known as "Lady of the Place of the Beginning of Time" and "One Who Was Before the Gods Were."

Sekhmet has always been recognized as a goddess of enormous power, a defender of the gods against all forces of evil. She is Lady of Flame, Great One of Magic, Sovereign of her father, Ra. The solar disc on her head signifies her control of the sun. As consort of her husband-brother Ptah, the creative process, Sekhmet is the one found most beautiful by Art itself.

It is said that no other Egyptian deity has been represented by so many statues. (A statue of her watches me always from the edge of my desk as I write.) The priests of Sekhmet were for centuries regarded as the most potent healers and magicians of the ancient world, due perhaps, to their utilization of the trance state.

It must be noted that Sekhmet has a dual nature. She is goddess of love and war, healing and pestilence, cursing and blessing.

In dealing with Sekhmet, one must maintain balance and emphasize the positive, for she has always been known as the most potentially dangerous of the Egyptian gods. Magicians and priests who seek her power know that the greatest source of all lies in Sekhmet. They also understand that they have nothing to fear as long as they emphasize their own positive aspects and do nothing to provoke her ferocious wrath.

It would seem that we humans are somehow always in a state of symbiosis with the world of the archetype. In that sense, then, the Egyptian gods retain their power and their energy to affect us and to interact with us. They are active symbols, still evolving with the consciousness of today's men and women.

RITES OF PREPARATION

For preparation rites more complex than pure meditation, you will have to use some of the tools on your altar. Let's return to Al Manning, Director of the ESP Lab in Los Angeles, for advice on proper consecration.

First of all, make sure that you have at least two candles, some protective incense [such as sandalwood], and vessels for earth, fire, and water. For added protection, mix a bit of salt with the water. It is also nice to have pieces of fresh, clean linen in which to wrap each article after its consecration.

For this ritual, Al suggests that you light the candles and the incense, then begin chanting aloud the following invocation to Shiva:

> Lovely, powerful Shiva,
> God of sweeping change,
> Sweep away the lesser,
> Shut it out of range.
> Leave the beauty and the Light,
> Bright and clean and fair.
> Remove all vibrations
> Of misery and despair.
> Leave this place and these fine things
> Fresh and bright and pure,
> Holy as your own fine self,
> Bright, complete and sure.
> Lovely, powerful Shiva,
> Our thanks to you we give.
> That from your sweeping power
> In beauty we may live.

This should be chanted from three to seven times--or however long it takes until you feel it has taken effect. When you feel comfortable, hold your vessel of water and salt in your hands, breathe in and out *as the water*. When you feel it breathing in your hands, chant softly:

> Water and salt, where you are cast
> No spell nor unknown purpose last
> Not in complete accord with me
> And as my will, so mote it be!

You are now holding, in essence, a glass of holy water, and it can be used to consecrate the other items on your altar. Dip your fingers into the vessel and lightly sprinkle the next object to be consecrated with the water. As you are doing this, invoke the water spirits to cast their protection upon the tools, catching the drops from your fingertips.

The best rituals are not the most arcane, or the ones discovered in some musty tome and scribbled in Hebrew. The best rituals are the ones to which you give the most energy and understand the best. These are most likely to be the ones you have devised yourself. Then you are not parroting someone else's words or stumbling over the pronounciation as you go; you are speaking with conviction from your own heart.

THE MAGICIAN'S CLOTHING

"If a magician of today were to construct special 'Sabbath garments' and consecrate them, he could either recite the names of the angels, as above, or throw in deities more personal to himself," the metaphysician Jeanyne has written. "A person well-versed in Greek or Roman 'mythology' may prefer to appeal to Apollo, god of light; Hera, goddess of the home; Athena, goddess of wisdom; Diana, goddess of chastity. All of these dominions have symbolic applications to innumerable personal quirks known only to the individual."

If we were to rewrite and update this ceremony, then, it might go something like this:

> *Isis, Ishtar, Demeter, Tiamet, Diana, Callieach. Macha;* by the virtue of these sacred names do I clothe myself, Great Mother, in my ritual garments, that in them I might fulfill all the desires I hope to effect from you; for you, mighty Goddess, are the source and sustenance of all living things. As my will, so mote it be.

OIL FOR ANOINTING

Jeanyne states that her altar is just at the right height so that she can sit cross-legged before it on the floor.

"Settle yourself according to your own arrangement," she advises, "then take one of your vessels, which has been filled with some kind of oil. You can make your own oils or you may use something like safflower or olive oil. Consecrate the oil as you did the salt water, and dip your fingers into it. Then anoint each of your seven psychic centers, which correspond to the endocrine gland system: the gonads, adrenals, thymus, thyroid, pineal, and pituitary glands.

"As you anoint yourself, say something like [feel free to develop your own]:

> "And now this oily essence fair
> Adds its great power to the air
> Attracting spirits of the Light
> Protecting us both day and night.
> This charge is true and proper, see
> And as my will, so mote it be!

"Or try something simple:

> "Diana, protectress of the innocent, with this oil may I purify and renew my purpose, that the deeds performed at this altar be for the good of all."

A RITUAL FOR REJUVENATION

In the April, 1969 issue of the newsletter *The Laughing Cat*, editor-publisher Leslie offers a relatively simple "Formula for Rejuvenation" which one might find useful if he be worn down by hostile psychic bombardment. This, Leslie's own magic formula, is based partly on a secret she discovered years ago, and partly on a rejuvenation secret taught her when she was but a young girl by a little gnome-like man.

> Put a green bulb in a lamp, and flood a darkened room with this soft green glow. Green is most soothing to both physical nerves and eyes.
>
> Begin with a tiny breath as you look at this green lamp-light and start breathing in bigger and deeper breaths, as you visualize yourself inwardly filling up with a burst of sparkling, emerald green light, from feet to top of head... This is lighting up your astral body with the Green, youthful and healing ray of astral electricity that indirectly heals,

intensifies and refreshes your physical body and mind.

Next, have a clear *green* glass of fresh water and sip it slowly, *feeling* the living magnetism of Life rushing all through you with every sip, 'til you have drained the glass.

...Now you are ready to lie down, flat on your back, legs and arms uncrossed. Relax, enjoy yourself for half an hour or an hour...in the mellow, life-giving green of this room. Imagine that you are floating in a world of *Green!*

Repeat this once every day. or night, for a week, then forget about it. After a week or more, do it again for another week...until you get results.

It is the greatest rest you could possibly get...Soon your face will look younger; you will feel refreshed, vitalized, full of energy.

HOW TO MAKE A "CURSE-REMOVING" PUPPET

If one is convinced that he has been cursed, he might enlist the aid of a Magi such as Cecil Williamson, who resides on Great Britain's Isle of Man.

"I only use magic for good purposes," Williamson stresses. He will not give medical advice to those who write to him for assistance. but he will attempt to aid afflicted clients by complicated rituals.

In many cases, Williamson says, he has no choice other than to fight evil (a very risky endeavor for the amateur, by the way). The general principle he uses in such a situation is to make an image, or puppet, to represent the one who has cast the malign spell.

In explaining a particular de-cursing ceremony. Williamson was quoted as saying: "For this, I used clay worked with water; the clay must come from a river and be worked with falling fresh water. Briefly, the other ingredients were salt-water worms for the intestines, pine gum for the sperm or essence of life in the body, the berry of ivy from a churchyard for the eyes, white quartz from a high cliff for the teeth, a pregnant brown rat, and a black cock, which were burned—they were dead, of course—on the altar of fire to the sun. There were several other more unpleasant substances in the puppet, but we need not go into every detail."

Williamson explained that such ingredients must be fresh for each molded puppet, and the search for traditional necessities and special herbs may keep him busy for most of a day. For the particular de-cursing which was witnessed by the journalist, Williamson required seed pods of woodruffe, toad flax, meadow saxifrage, earth nut, and devil's bit. He pointed out that a less reliable member of his profession might have cancelled out the effects of the spell by carelessly omitting a required ingredient or by unprofessionally substituting one herb for another.

Once Williamson has fashioned a puppet, he subjects it to an arcane ritual and mails it to his client. Careful instructions for its use are included in its box.

In one case, a client was advised to bury the box containing the puppet under a thin layer of soil. Over the soil, the client was told to light a bonfire and to add his own curses while the fire burned. Such an act, Williamson explained to his client, would intensify and renew the force of the fire which he had burned within his magic circle on the Isle of Man.

An incantation which Williamson often sends along with a curse-removing puppet goes like this:

> Blow, blow, blow
> Spirit of the North Winds;
> Blow, blow, blow,
> Spirit of the East Winds.
> Nourish and feed this fire,
> Make fire become furnace,
> To burn and utterly consume
> The one who ill-wishes me.

The Magi has emphasized that such a counter-curse, to be really effective, should be repeated several times over with ever-increasing force, power, and vehemence until the fire has burned itself out or the client has worn himself out with repeating the curses.

DO-IT-YOURSELF EXORCISM

If one should feel that he has really caught himself a hex, the two most powerful methods of counteracting sorcery are prayer and exorcism. Prayers, amulets, symbols, charms, and so forth, call for the exercise of will, mental concentration. Exorcism is the method by which evil spirits are bound by a Priest by means of ceremonies and formulas, and cast away, or out of, the accursed.

Rollo Ahmed has offered procedures of a number of exorcisms by which evil forces might be resisted.

Ahmed tells us that only a priest or someone well-versed in the Occult should attempt an exorcism.

In one method, Ahmed prescribes sealing the entrance to the house of the accursed one with wax made with wafers of the Host. Chalk crosses should be drawn on all the doors, and frankincense should be burnt over a large fire. A small portion of this fire is to be placed in a senser and carried from room to room at the same time that the exorcist prays for a hasty departure of evil. When this step has been completed, Holy Water that has been consecrated in a church is to be sprinkled about the rooms of the house by means of a hyssop.

The words, "I exorcise thee, O unclean spirit, in the name of the Father and of the Son and of the Holy Ghost," must be repeated in each room of the afflicted party's home. If a violent physical manifestation should occur, Ahmed advises, the exorcist should demand the source of the evil.

Among several methods of driving away evil forces, Ahmed gives one wherein the hexed individual might conduct the ceremony of exorcism by himself.

First a room should be selected for the ritual and it must be thoroughly cleaned. Only the most essential furniture should remain. If space limitations prevent one's removing the furniture, the pieces should be pushed back against the walls as far as possible.

The person seeking the purification should next have a bath, preferably in cold water, and then put on clean clothes (most desirable would be a white robe especially made for the occasion).

Seven small brass bowls are to be arranged at intervals so that they form a circle roughly nine feet in diameter (if one is cramped for room, six feet will suffice). The bowls are to be filled with charcoal, sprinkled with frankincense, and should be allowed to burn while the officiator takes his place at the lower edge of the circle, either standing or sitting cross-legged and facing North or East.

We shall visualize our officiator sitting crosslegged as it would seem that most people would prefer this position. In front of him should be two bowls filled with water—a large one on his left, a smaller one to his right. Directly in front of the larger bowl should be three candlesticks bearing unlit candles.

Although it is not absolutely necessary, it would be best if the base of the candlesticks should have star-like three, five, or eight points. According to the inclination of the officiator, the candlesticks may be arranged in either a straight line or a triangular formation. Incense sticks should also be burnt within the circle to add to the aroma of the frankincense.

Ahmed recommends 11:00 A.M. as the best time for the ritual, but states that 11:00 P.M. may also be set as the appointed hour. Some authorities suggest a darkened room, but Ahmed believes a fully lighted area serves the purposes of exorcism much better.

Upon his entering the circle, the officiator is to recite the following:

"I invoke the powers of light and the powers of love, and the purifying spirit that is in fire, and in water, to gather around me their forces and protection."

The officiator is to pause for about three minutes, then continue the invocation:

"I call upon all the higher spiritual forces and beings who have the progress and welfare of their human brothers in their care, to be witness to the promise (or vow) that I am about to make to cast away those things that are unworthy and to release the spirit within, and thus become impervious to any evil vibrations that may be seeking to harm me. I renounce _____(whatever evil or fault is required to banish; such as pride, vanity, lust, intemperance, etc.), which forms a link with evil forces."

The officiator pauses, then recites the Lord's Prayer, taking care to say, "L*eave us not when in* temptation," instead of "L*ead us not into* temptation."

Now, having renounced evil and recited the Lord's Prayer, the officiator should light the candles and drink a portion of the water in the smaller bowl.

A five-minute meditation period on peace and harmony should be next observed. At the conclusion of the meditation, the officiator should dip his fingers in the larger bowl of water and shake them three times.

The officiator now leaves the circle, taking the larger bowl of water with him. The contents of the bowl are emptied, but the circle and the rest of the articles within it are to remain untouched. The candles should be permitted to burn down; the frankincense and incense should smolder until self-consumed.

Under no circumstances is the officiator to re-enter the circle, and the door to the room is to remain locked until the next day.

If this ritual can only be performed at night, Ahmed cautions, on no account must the officiator use a red light to supplement the light of the candles. It would be best if the ceremony were conducted by candlelight alone, but blue or green lights may be used.

The officiator must take care to sit as quietly as possible when he is within the magic circle. Any nervous fidgeting can cause disharmony and weaken the vibrations.

Only if the officiator is mentally distressed should another person be present to witness the ceremony. In most cases, the officiator should be alone.

The ritual may also be used to drive away evil from a "haunted house" if the sentence "I renounce _____ which forces a link with evil forces," be changed to "I exorcise the evil influence and dispel the dark forces within this house."

If the officiator should be nervous about using fire in the ceremony, the same ritual could be performed by substituting flowers for flames and seven white glass vases for the seven brass bowls. If at all possible, the flowers should be handpicked by the officiator himself. Their colors may be white, blue, mauve, pink, or mixed, but they must never be red.

In the event that flowers should be used by the officiator, the circle is to be broken at the completion of the ceremony by removing the seven vases of flowers and placing them in a straight row in another part of the room. The room must remain locked, as in the fire ceremony, and at the end of the twenty-four hour period, the flowers must either be burned or buried.

Under no circumstances are they to be used in another part of the house or to be given to someone else. A simple toss in the garbage will not do, either. They must be consumed by flame or given back to the earth.

YOUR OWN CRUSADER'S SWORD TO WARD OFF EVIL

In his *Book of Legendary Spells*, Elbee Wright includes an ancient ritual for warding off evil.

The operator faces the East and makes the sign of the Cabalistic Cross. As he touches his forehead, he whispers, "Thou art;" as he touches his solar plexus, he says, "Thy Kingdom;" as he touches his right shoulder, he says, "and the Power;" as he touches his left shoulder, he says, "and the Glory." Then, with hands clasped, he says loudly, "Amen!"

Wright explains that the Cabalistic Cross is not only a religious cross, but also includes the Occult symbolism for the four elements of Fire, Water, Earth and Air, and the four Quarters of the Earth.

Once he has made the sign of the Cabalistic Cross, the operator should visualize a huge, Crusader's sword upraised in his right hand. While concentrating on the sword, he should say: "In the name of the Supreme Lord God, I raise in defiance of Satan and his legions and against all malefactors, the Sword of Strength and Peace."

This said, and still concentrating on the huge mental sword clutched in his right hand, the operator is to picture himself as twice his height, a powerful, massive, tower of supreme power and irresistible strength.

Once this has been accomplished, the operator lowers the Crusader's sword and begins to draw a mental circle about himself. He should visualize a golden flame at the point of his sword that leaves a circle of flickering light as he moves the blade about him.

At this point, the operator eliminates the visualized sword and concentrates on the burning circle of light that surrounds him.

Now, raising his clasped and prayerful hands above his head, the operator faces East and says:

"I pray and trust that the mighty archangel Raphael will protect me from all evil forces and demons approaching from the East."

Immediately, he faces South and utters the same prayer, this time invoking the name of Michael rather than Raphael. When he prays to the West, Gabriel is invoked, and to the North, the angel Uriel. At the time that he once again faces the East, the sign of the Cabalistic Cross is repeated.

The adherents of White Magic believe that this spell will protect anyone within its circle for either the twelve hours of day or the twelve hours of night. It is deemed especially valuable for protecting the sleeper, for he may visualize the golden, fiery circle encompassing the entire bedroom. The process may be intensified by the burning of incense in a bowl in the center of the envisioned golden circle of fire.

CHAPTER TWELVE: USING CRYSTALS FOR HIGH MAGIC

Creating the Perfect You through Crystal Power
Improving Your Love-Making Abilities
The Aztec Ritual of Astral Projection
A Crystal Past Lives Scan
Summoning the Spirit Teacher
Using Your Crystal to Banish Evil and Negativity
Explore the Future with Crystal Vision
The Crystal Capstone on the Pyramid of Love
Focusing the Divine Fire
Travel to Outer Space in Your Own Crystal Starship

IT is a tradition among the Native Medicine People that a crystal to be used for healing should be given to you. Interestingly, it was during one of our very first meetings that Frances presented me with the quartz crystal that I have now utilized in my meditations and healing sessions for the past twelve years. The other that I employ was given to me by a healer from North Carolina.

This is not to say, of course. that you cannot go out and purchase a crystal on your own in the event that none of your friends are yet aware of the power of crystals in New Age Magick.

The exercises in this chapter should be approached with utmost seriousness of purpose, for they all involve High Magick. They will be drawing upon the maximum of your inner resources.

Believe me, though, the results which you can achieve if you apply yourself with all sincerity will produce profound insights and will manifest miraculous changes in your life pattern.

Since this is a book of practical applications, rather than theory, I shall not take the time to regale you with accounts of the scientific research that is presently being conducted to validate the remarkable power of crystals.

Suffice it to remind you that our first radio sets were crystal "receiving sets," that the major component of watches is a crystal, that crystal serves as the memory bank in computers, and that the human body, being 78-96 percent water, is actually a liquid crystal.

CREATING THE PERFECT YOU THROUGH CRYSTAL POWER

Yes, it is true: You can use your crystal to enable you to achieve any body shape that you wish. It doesn't matter if you want to be fashion-model-slim or pinup girl curvaceous. It doesn't matter if you want to be lean and mean or bulk up like Hercules. All it takes to create the body shape of your dreams is your willingness to practice crystal power and your commitment to stick to a steady program of exercise.

Yes, I said exercise. You cannot remain a couch potato and a lounge lizard and expect the crystal to do all the work. If you don't feel that you can discipline yourself enough to work up a sweat and to engage in a regimen of physical conditioning, you had better skip this particular program. But if you wish to be a commanding New Age Magician in body (as well as in mind and spirit), if you wish to enjoy the benefits of good health and endurance. then read on and begin to shape the Perfect You.

Take your crystal in your left hand. Holding the crystal in your left hand will stimulate the creative, intuitive process in the right brain hemisphere. The vortex of energy in the crystal will now begin interacting with your own electromagnetic field and will start to increase the field energy around you.

Now begin to breathe into your crystal your *intention* to shape your physical body exactly the way you ideally wish it to be. The thing to remember is that the crystal will magnify your intention.

Sit quietly in a place where you will be undisturbed by all external stimuli for at least thirty minutes. Calm yourself and attempt to clear your mind of all troublesome thoughts.

Take a comfortably deep breath, hold it for the count of three, then exhale slowly. Take another comfortably deep breath, hold it for the count of four, exhale slowly. And then a third comfortably deep breath, hold it for the count of five, exhale very slowly.

Accept that you have within you a Higher Self that is the ultimate you. This Higher Self is a magnificent blueprint of your perfect self, the very image of that which you have the potential to become.

Form a mental picture of yourself as your Higher Self. See yourself exactly as you *know* you have the potential to become. Place your crystal in the "third eye" area in the center of your forehead and hold the image of your Higher Self.

The mental picture of your perfect self must make *no* reference to the way that you *now* appear. You must only focus on your perfect self as you wish yourself to be. You must not visualize at any time your body build as it is at the present time.

If you send a thoughtform to your Higher Self which includes a mental "photograph" of the way you look now, it is as if you are sending "before" and "after" pictures. The result will be a muddle.

You must believe that within your Higher Self is the true image of your perfect self. And you must hold the thought of how you envision your perfect self to be.

Once you have fashioned that image of your perfect physical self, hold it fast and begin to breathe in very slowly, taking comfortably deep breaths. As you inhale. you are drawing in what some mystics refer to as the *mana* and what martial artists refer to as the *ki or the chi*, the all-pervasive life force. The same unknown energy that permits them to smash boards and bricks with their bare hands will also allow you to shape the body image of your choice.

Make and memorize the picture of your perfect self as you breathe and draw in the *mana*. It is the mana that will give the picture enough strength to hold together while the High Self begins to materialize the image into physical actuality for your. Hold the picture firmly in your mind as you continue to breathe slowly and to send energy to the Higher Self.

L*ive* in the picture.

F*eel* it.

Keep your mind from all negative thoughts to the contrary.

VISUALIZING THE PERFECT YOU

Lower your left hand with your crystal to your side and settle yourself in a position in which you can become completely relaxed.

You may read the following visualization, pausing now and then to reflect upon the process. Or you may wish to have a friend read the techniques to you as you relax and experience the imagery.

TRANSPARENT QUARTZ
FROM CRYSTAL MOUNTAIN, GARLAND COUNTY, ARK.

You must always remember to breathe your intention into your crystal before seriously beginning any exercise.

It is also possible to record your own voice, reading this exercise into a tape recorder, so that you may play the tape back and allow your voice to guide you through the relaxation process and through the procedure.

Any of the above methods can be effective. Just be certain that you are at a time and in a place where you will not be disturbed for at least thirty minutes.

Your success in this exercise depends upon your willingness to permit a transformation to manifest in your consciousness. As an additional aid to the process, you might play some inspirational or stirring background music to heighten the effect. Be certain, though, that the music contains no lyrics to distract you.

THE "FLOATING CLOUD" TECHNIQUE OF RELAXATION

Permit yourself to relax...totally and completely.

Lie back in a comfortable position and release all worries...all tensions...all problems. Let your mind float. Relax...relax. Take three comfortably deep breaths and relax.

Imagine before you now the softest, fluffiest cloud in the sky. See it settling down next to you as you relax...relax. See yourself crawling upon it to rest...to float...to relax...to rise to the sky and leave all your problems behind you...leave all your tensions behind you.

Float and drift, drift and float, rising to the sky in a comfortable slow, swinging motion. Nothing will disturb you. Nothing will distress you. No sound will bother you. In fact, should you hear any sound at all, that sound will only help you to relax. Take three more comfortably deep breaths...and relax.

You are floating up into the sky, drifting higher and higher. You feel safe and totally secure. It is impossible for you to fall. Feel peace and contentment. Drift...and float. Drift and float. You are entering a feeling of total peace and total relaxation.

As you are drifting and floating with your mind completely at peace, you are aware that your body has been rising higher and higher. You have been comfortably soaring through the clouds, and the higher you float, the less you are aware of any stress or tension. All of your body is completely relaxed. Your toes...feet...legs... torso...arms, shoulders...neck...all are totally relaxed.

Now you are aware of a great bolt of electrical energy that is shooting toward you. You know that it will not harm you in any way. It will, in fact, energize you.

It will energize you and give you strength and power. It will give you strength and power to mold and to shape your body any way that you most desire it to be.

Feel the soothing, yet exhilerating, warmth as this bolt of power touches your body. Feel the warm, tingling energy moving throughout your entire body. Feel the energy moving down your spine, bringing great strength and power to your entire being. Feel the energy gathering in your arms, your back, your chest, your legs.

You are now aware of another great bolt of electrical energy shooting toward you. It is another Lightning Bolt of Strength and Power. You feel its warm energy touching you. Two powerful surges of energy course through your body, and you are aware of great strength building in each of your muscles.

And now a *third* Lightning Bolt of Strength and Power touches and activates you with incredible energy. You can feel a mounting surge of strength multiplying within each of your muscles. Waves of pleasure and anticipation course through your entire being. You are pulsating with power and energy.

You are now ready to begin your physical exercises. You are surging with power such as you have never before experienced. You cannot wait to begin to work the muscles in your arms, your chest, your legs...your entire body.

You will be stronger than you have ever been. You will give full expression to the Lightning Bolt of Strength and Power. You feel throbbing, synchronized energy rhythmically pulsating deep within your being, your very essence.

And as you perform each of your sets and your repetitions, you will visualize your muscles growing exactly as you wish them to grow. You will see your body shaping itself, molding itself, to the image that you fashion within your mind. You will see every muscle in your body responding to your will.

Each and every cell within your body will obey your commands to shape, to mold, to sculpture muscles *exactly* as you envision them. Each and every cell within your body will obey your mental commands to shape, to mold, to sculpture *precisely* the physical image, the body image, that you most desire.

Now you may begin your workout. It will be as it has never been before. You will be perfect, magnificent in each set, each individual repetition. Your strength and power will be the wonder and the envy of all who behold you. At the count of *three*, you will emerge from this state of relaxation eager to enter the gym and to begin your workout.

One...eager to begin to workout and to shape your body as you wish it.

Two...each cell, fiber, and muscle ready to be molded and shaped.

Three...charged with the Lightning Bolt of Strength and Power. Strong as never before!

Awaken!

IMPROVING YOUR LOVE-MAKING ABILITIES

Prepare yourself precisely as you did for the previous exercise. Remember to hold your crystal in your left hand and to breathe your intention into it.

The Floating Cloud technique of relaxation should also be the same. We now begin the technique for Improving Your Love-making Abilities at the point when either a friend or your own prerecorded voice has progressed you well into a relaxed state of consciousness:

As you are drifting and floating with your mind completely at peace, you are aware that your body has been rising higher and higher, comfortably soaring through the clouds. The higher you rise, the less you are aware of your physical body. All of your body is completely relaxed. Your toes...feet...legs... torso...arms...shoulders...neck...are totally relaxed. You remain aware only of your mind...and your sex organs.

Now you are aware of a great bolt of electrical energy that is shooting toward you. You know that it will not harm you in any way. It will, in fact, energize you. It will energize you and give you power. It is the Lightning Bolt of Sexual Power.

Feel the soothing warmth of this bolt of sensual pleasure as it touches your body. Feel the warm, tingling energy moving throughout your entire body. You feel the energy moving through your brain, and you feel your unconscious level of reality becoming activated. You sense the energy moving down your spine, bringing power into your entire being. You feel the energy gathering in your sexual organs.

Now you are aware of another great bolt of electrical energy shooting toward you. It is the Lighting Bolt of Sensual Pleasure. You feel its warm energy touching you, and you sense it moving to the very center of your psyche, activating the left side of your brain, your conscious reality. Two powerful surges of energy course through your body, and you are aware of the exuberant warmth moving into your sex organs, filling the regions with strength and power.

All the energy of your body and the electricity from the Lightning Bolt of Sensual Pleasure are now centered in your sex organs. Feel them becoming activated, throbbing with excitement.

And now once again you receive a bolt of lightning. You have received a charge from the Lightning Bolt of Sexual Ability. You can feel a mounting surge of energy begin to multiply within you. Feel that energy throb deep within your sex organs. The warmth feels so good, so pleasurable.

Feel the heat rising, sending exciting waves of pleasure throughout your entire being. Feel yourself begin to pulsate with all the energy that your mind and body can generate. A heightened state of ecstasy is mounting higher and higher. You feel almost blinded by the glowing energy around you. Every cell in your body is vibrating.

The power of sensual energy permeates your entire being, sending waves of pleasure through your loins... your thighs...your chest...your entire body. Feel the throbbing, synchronized energy rhythmically pulsating deep within your being, your essence.

The Three Lightning Bolts of Sexual Energy have filled your body with incredible power. Your inner vision has become crystal clear. Your hearing is keener, sharper, than it has ever been before in your life. Your sense of touch is more sensitive than you knew was possible. Your nostrils are experiencing aromas far beyond the normal spectrum.

You are hearing sounds that only a great jungle cat could hear. You are seeing, touching, smelling, feeling sensations that only a powerful jungle cat could experience. Enjoy the muscular sensation. Feel the sleek power of the jungle cat that you are.

Now you are sensing a jungle cat of the opposite sex. You are hungry for its presence as you move lithely, effortlessly through the jungle brush and foliage. Your powerful body is sinewy and strong. You are a magnificent jungle cat, and you have enormous strength and power to mate with another.

You hear a rustling in the grass. You smell and sense a lover approaching you in the darkness. You see smoldering eyes looking at you from the shadows. A full moon overhead casts mysterious silhouettes that will enhance your lovemaking. You feel desire rising high within you.

A sensual purr sounds from within the other's throat. It is an invitation for you to make love. Your muscles become hard, more pronounced. You feel a surge of power. Blood courses through your body, your legs, filling you with a pounding need.

Only one thought consumes you: Enjoy animal pleasure. Feel and enjoy the sensation of your loins throbbing, burning with pent up desire. Feel wild, uninhibited.

Your head, your mind, your body, your loins are all one. Feel your entire body throbbing. You are one with the energy. You are one with sensual pleasure. You are one with your partner.

When you have enjoyed all that you desire to experience, you have the ability to return to your normal state, knowing that you can return to this pleasurable state of being by saying over and over the word, "power." All that you need to do to become this sensual jungle cat again is to take three deep breaths and say softly, "Power. Power. Power." At that time you will feel the strength, the power, and the sexual energy surge throughout your entire body.

Now you are coming back to the present reality. You are coming back to your reality as a human being named _____(say your name). At the count of five, you will return feeling better than you have in weeks and weeks. At the count of five, you will return filled with the awareness of sensual power. You will return filled with the sexual energy of the jungle cat.

You are now coming awake: *One*...feeling very good in mind and body. *Two*...remembering the activating word, "*Power.*" *Three*...Feeling confident...strong. *Four*... "*Power*..."*Power.*" *Five*...wide awake and feeling great.

Some Additional Tips

The first step should be practiced seriously until you definitely feel yourself receiving an energy peak. You should practice this visualization until you feel your body filled with sexual power. Diligent practice on a daily basis can aid even the most difficult sexual problems.

The second step, becoming one with the powerful imagery of a great jungle cat, is important in order to provide you with a firm foundation upon which to build your sexual fantasies. You should come to visualize so clearly that you actually feel as though you have become that jungle cat. Your visualization should be so precise that you can really see that thick jungle brush and foliage and feel like a great cat readying itself for a total sexual experience.

The more you practice, the more intense will become the programming of the activating word *"Power"* to trigger a transformation in your love-making.

Once you have become quite proficient at the jungle cat *personna*, expand your visualizations to include scenarios which feature any other animal that might appeal to you.

THE AZTEC RITUAL OF ASTRAL PROJECTION

This exercise will require two crystals, one somewhat larger than the other. You must also have a candle in a sturdy holder.

Hold the crystal with which you feel "friendliest" on the intuitive level in your left hand. Lightly touch the tips of the two crystals and permit the energy fields to interact.

As this is being accomplished, lean forward and breathe your intention to astral project into the crystals. Repeat this process of intention three times.

Set the larger crystal aside and place the smaller crystal in your left hand (if it is not already there). Hold the crystal so that you can see the flame of the candle dancing in its interior. Mentally draw in the energy of the fire.

Place the crystal over your "third eye," directly in the center of your forehead.

The following visualization should now be read by a trusted friend or you may previously have spoken the process in your own voice and preserved the technique on a tape recorder. Be certain that you are at a time and in a place where you will not be disturbed for at least thirty minutes.

Your success in this exercise depends upon your willingness to permit a transformation to manifest in your consciousness. New Age music, such as that performed by Stephen Halpern or Michael Stearn can truly heighten the demonstration.

You may use the "floating cloud" method of relaxation described in the "Perfect You" exercise or you may utilize any other technique of quieting the consciousness that has been successful for you. Once the body has been relaxed, proceed with the following visualization:

You are seeing memory patterns before you. They may be your memories of a past life experience. They may be the memories of another. It does not matter. You are seeing them form before you now.

Two crystals are necessary for the preliminary states of the Aztec Astral Projection technique.

The memories are taking you to a faraway place, a faraway time on the vibration of the Eternal Now. You are seeing blue, blue sky. Mountains. A city made of stone high in the mountains. An inner awareness tells you where you are. You are in Peru. The Andes Mountains. You are remembering an ancient city there.

You are remembering that you were a student there, a very special student of a very special teacher--a priest, a master, a wizard. He stands before you now in a colorful robe fashioned from the feathers of a hundred different birds.

This priest, this master-teacher, has made you his prize pupil. You, more than any of the other initiates, have responded perfectly to his teachings. When the master-teacher and other priests utter a certain sound or give you a special signal, you are able to leave your body. When the master-teacher transmits to you a secret sign, you soar free of your physical limitations. You soar high above the Earth. You soar free of Time and Space. You can go anywhere you wish--instantly. You have but to think it...and you will be there.

You are proud that you have become your master's special student. You are proud that of all the students in the class, you are the one who has been selected for the great demonstration.

And even now you are walking through a path, surrounded by the other students. It is night. There is a full moon. You are walking to a place where you will give the demonstration. Look around you. Remember the faces of those nearest you. Remember the faces of those standing watching you. Remember everything you see around you.

Now you are approaching the area of the demonstration. You see your master-teacher, the High Priest, is already there. His robe is blowing gently in a breeze. On either side of him stands a priest.

Twelve students step forward from the crowd and form a circle around a blanket that has been spread on the ground. You step into the circle, advance to the blanket. You take a deep breath and lie down on the blanket. You look up at the full Moon A small cloud moves across its face. You lie quietly for a few moments, then raise an arm to signal that you are ready.

You lie there on the blanket, on your back, looking up at the full Moon. You are calm. You are relaxed. You know that when you hear or see the secret signal, you will soar free of your body. Your essential self, the REAL YOU that exists within, will burst free of the limitations of the physical body and shoot up toward the sky, toward the Moon.

The High Priest, your master-teacher, gives you the signal. NOW!

You feel yourself rushing, pushing, pulsating, spinning ...bursting free of the body!

You, the Real You, soars toward the Moon. Down below you can see the students, the priests, your master-teacher. But your universe is only you and your spirit projection.

Go wherever you wish. You have but to think it and you will be there...INSTANTLY.

Think of a loved one...a loved one who is faraway. You have but to think of that loved one and you will be there...INSTANTLY. You will be beside that loved one INSTANTLY.

Think of a place--a city, a forest, a desert, an ocean--anywhere. Think of that place, and you will be there. INSTANTLY.

Go wherever you wish--free of Time and Space. You will return to full consciousness when you have seen what it is that you are supposed to perceive.

A CRYSTAL PAST LIVES SCAN

For this revealing past lives scan you will require your crystal, a candle, a stick of incense, and some artifacts that represent the past. You will notice in the photograph accompanying this chapter that I am using a statue of Sekhmet and a figure of an owl to represent the ancient wisdoms. Sandalwood is my favorite scent, but you must feel free to select whichever incense most triggers your own intuitive faculties.

Grasp your crystal in your left hand. Breathe your intention to gain meaningful glimpses into past lives into your crystal. Repeat the process three times.

Hold your crystal at eye level and begin to gaze into it in the classic "crystal ball" attitude. Continue to stare into the crystal as either a friend or your own prerecorded voice reads the following visualization to your.

Keep your eyes open, looking intently into the crystal, until your lids begin to feel heavy. Permit your eyes to close naturally, when they wish to shut out external distractions, and lower your crystal when it begins to feel "heavy."

Be certain that you have completed a total relaxation technique before you begin the visualization process.

You may utilize the "floating cloud" technique described earlier.

The Past Lives Scan

A purple mist is moving up around you. It is the purple mist of Time. You know that you have the ability to see and to scan all of Time. You will be able to feel which periods of Time attract you the most. As the purple mist moves up around you, you are beginning to scan all of Time. You are moving farther and farther back in Time...

The purple mist comes up around you and you find yourself in a scene from another past life experience. You are witnessing yourself in a scene from a lifetime in which you had a deep and meaningful relationship with your parents.

A man and a woman are approaching you. Look into those eyes. Feel the love from those eyes.

And now. looking deeply into those eyes, see if you have come together with that man and that woman again in your present life experience. For your good and your gaining, see if you have come together again to complete a lesson left unlearned, to finish some work left undone.

Look at the eyes of the woman, and you will know. Look at the eyes of the man, and you will know. They may not have come this time as your parents, but as a friend, a teacher, a relative, a business associate, or, perhaps, even one of your own children. But look into the eyes and you will know. You will know if they have returned to complete a circle of love with you.

And now in that same lifetime, you are watching another person coming toward you. It may be a man or it may be a woman. But you are looking at the eyes, and you see that it is a brother or a sister from that same life experience.

It may be a brother or a sister with whom you had a deep and beautiful relationship. It may be a brother or a sister with whom you had a conflict. a misunderstanding, a deep-seated quarrel.

But you are looking at the eyes, and you will know. You will know if that brother or that sister has come with you again to complete a lesson left unlearned, to finish some work left undone. Look at the eyes, and you will know if that person has come with you in your present life experience.

You are now seeing the Purple Mist coming up around you again, and you are viewing a scene from a lifetime

in which you had to struggle against great odds in order to achieve a meaningful goal. Everything that you see will be for your good and your gaining. Nothing will disturb you. Nothing will distress you. You will be able to see everything from a detached and unemotional point of view.

You may be seeing yourself in a work situation, a political situation, a scene of strife; you may even be seeing yourself fighting in a war, but you are seeing the scene clearly. You are seeing it for your good and your gaining. You are detached, unemotional.

You are now seeing a friend or a loved one who supported you throughout your great struggle. This is one who was always there, who never failed you. Look deep into the loving eyes of that one who always loved and supported you. For your good and your gaining, see if that friend, that loved one, came with you in your present life experience, to complete a lesson left unlearned, to finish work left undone. Look into the eyes, and you will know.

And now you are looking into the eyes of one who steadfastly opposed you in that lifetime. This is one who tried to block everything you attempted. Look into those eyes, deep into those eyes, and for your good and your gaining, see if that one who opposed you came with you in your present life experience, to complete a lesson left unlearned, to finish work left undone. Look into the eyes, and you will know. And now, for your good and your gaining, see if you attained your goal!

Now you are moving through the purple mist of Time to another past life experience, you are moving to view a scene from a past life when you had very special abilities, very special abilities. Some may even have called you a witch, a wizard, a sorceror. This was a past life in which you exercised great control over the X FORCE, the Unknown Energy.

See WHERE you went to learn these special abilities.

See HOW you acquired them.

See FROM WHOM you acquired these very special abilities. Look deep into those eyes, and for your good and your gaining, see if that person has come with you in your present life experience, to complete a lesson left unlearned, to finish work undone.

And now. most importantly, see HOW you used your special abilities. Did you use them for good...or for negativity? See, now, clearly, what special lesson you learned from that life experience.

Columba Krebs

Gaze into your crystal and visualize images moving forward from the Purple Mist of Time.

A brilliant ray of sunlight shines through the purple mist of Time, and you find yourself in a past life experience in which you had a powerful, beautiful love relationship. See now as that person approaches you again. Feel the love coming from those eyes.

Feel the eyes of that beloved one upon you again. This is one who loved you so deeply, so intensely. This is one who was always there when you needed love and support, when you needed someone to hold you.

This is the one who was always there to dry your tears, to hold you close and whisper, "It's all right. Everything will be all right. As long as we are always together."

And now you look deep into the eyes of that beloved one as you feel once again those wonderful arms move around you, those lips touching your own.

Look deeply into those eyes and, for your good and your gaining, see if that beloved one has come with you again, to complete a lesson left unlearned, to finish work left undone.

See if this beloved one has come to you again. See if you were born again to be together. See if you have come together again to complete a beautiful cycle of love. Look into those eyes, and you will know.

Look into the eyes, and you will know.

And you are coming awake. The purple mist of time is leaving you.

You are coming awake with remembrance of all you need to know for your good and your gaining.

You are feeling wonderful both in body and in mind. You are coming awake filled with love and filled with full remembrance of all you need to remember for your good and your gaining. Awaken!

SUMMONING THE SPIRIT TEACHER

Hold your crystal in your lefthand. You should be seated comfortably in a place and at a time when you will not be disturbed for at least thirty minutes. Inspirational music playing in the background usually proves to be of great benefit in accelerating the awesome experience of encountering your loving, benevolent Spirit Teacher.

Breathe your intention to meet your Spirit Teacher into the crystal. Repeat the process three times.

Bring the crystal before your eyes as close as you can without blurring your vision or making yourself uncomfortable. Visualize that you can see within the crystal another world, another dimension. Perceive spires, turrets, temples, streets. A beautiful Crystal City. Play with this notion for a few moments before you begin the process of relaxation.

Your success in this very important exercise depends upon your desire to make contact with the multidimensional being that serves as your Spirit Teacher. **Be certain that you are in an extremely relaxed state before the voice of a friend—or your own prerecorded voice— leads you through the following process:**

As your body lies now in a deep sleep, your mind, your Essential Self, is very much aware that you are being surrounded by a beautiful golden light, and you feel the warmth of the light from the source of All-That-Is beginning to stimulate your Crown Chakra.

You are becoming one with the feeling of being loved unconditionally by an intelligence who has always loved you just as you are.

Now you are sensing the presence of an intelligence that you have always known on one level of consciousness. You have known that this intelligence has been near you ever since you were a child.

You are becoming aware of the sensation of warmth in both your Heart Chakra and your Crown Chakra. You are aware of a ray of light that is connecting your essence to the higher vibrations of this entity—this light being that is approaching you.

Now you are seeing that the golden light has acquired a tinge of pink. See it begin to swirl around you, moving faster and faster until it begins to acquire a form and substance. Now you see the shape of a body, of hair, of a beautiful smile and a loving face.

You are becoming especially aware of the eyes. You feel the love, the unconditional love, that flows out to you from those eyes. You feel yourself becoming even more enveloped in the warmth of unconditional love from this higher intelligence that is approaching.

You are aware in your inner self that, materializing before you now, is the image of your spiritual guide. You have an inner knowing that your guide has come to take you to a special place where you will be able to receive profound and meaningful visions designed to aid you to achieve your fullest good and your utmost gaining.

Your guide stretches forth a firm, but loving, hand. Take that hand in your own.

Feel the love flowing through you. Feel the vibration of one who has always loved you. Feel the vibration of love from one who has loved you with pure, heavenly.

unconditional love. Feel the vibration of one who has come to take you to a special place where profound visions await you.

You see a purple mist clouding up around you as you begin to move through Time and Space with your spiritual guide.

Now you are seeing yourself in a holy place.

You may be seeing yourself in a beautiful garden that lies before a majestic temple.

You may be seeing yourself in a magic place in a forest.

You may be seeing yourself high on some mountain retreat.

You may be remembering a scene from a past life experience in which you devoted yourself to spiritual service. You may be remembering a life as a monk, a nun, a priest, a medicine man or woman, a yogi, a high priestess.

Whatever you might have been, you remember this holy place that now appears before you.

There is now a vibration in the air as if bells are chiming. At that sound, at that signal, a wise teacher comes to meet you.

See the love in those eyes as the teacher sees you. Look deeply into the eyes of that beloved teacher. As you do so you will learn the name of this great master teacher.

Become totally aware of your spiritual teacher. See his clothes, his body, his face, his eyes, his mouth, the way he holds his hands.

The teacher tells you that he has a gift of greeting for you. He says it is a very special gift that will aid you in achieving a deep and powerful vision.

He reaches within his robe and brings forth a leather bag. He opens the leather bag and hands you the gift.

You look at the gift. See what it is. Take the gift. Feel it. Know it. Tell the teacher how you feel about him and his gift.

Now you are once again aware that your spiritual guide is beside you. Your guide has taken your hand to walk beside you and the master teacher.

The three of you are now walking in a tunnel. The master teacher is leading you to a secret place.

As you walk, you turn to your spiritual guide and you say, "Oh, guide, one who has loved me and cared for me since before my awareness, please tell me what your name is."

If it is to be at this time, your guide will reveal the name by which you might summon his vibration again--

the name by which you might call upon this source of strength.

Experience your emotions as you walk between your guide and your master teacher. Feel deeply your expectations.

See the torches set into the walls. Be aware of any aromas, any sounds, any sights.

You are now in a great room. Look around you slowly. See statues and paintings arranged around the room. See them and remember them.

Your spiritual teacher is now showing you a great crystal that is supported on a golden tripod. As you lean forward to stare into the crystal, your spiritual teacher tells you that he will now permit you to see a meaningful vision.

He tells you that you will now see all that you need to see at this time for your good and your gaining. You will see all that is necessary for your present level of understanding. You will see a vision that will be completely individualized for you and for your particular needs.

See that vision now!

USING YOUR CRYSTAL TO BANISH EVIL AND NEGATIVITY

By focusing the Violet Light of Transmutation through your crystal, you can accomplish the welcome act of banishing negativity from your life. The following exercises should be practiced with a smaller crystal that you can carry with you at all times.

Dealing With Negativity

Understand that your spiritual guide directs the Violet Light of Transmutation from the Divine Fire. The violet light is the highest vibratory level in the spectrum of light vibration. Summoning the violet light can assist you in balancing the negativity that you may have sown or may have directed against yourself. By earnestly manifesting the violet light you will be able to eliminate any negativity in your life.

Certain great spiritual masters liken the violet light to an eraser. When you learn to use it often and opportunely, you may erase all from your spiritual spectrum that is not of the Divine Light.

Other teachers have said that the violet light may be used to dissolve disease, to eliminate suffering, to cure illness. Disease, suffering, and illness are all manifestations of chaos and discord. Suffusing them with a violet light may alter them and raise their vibratory levels to points of transmutation.

Know and understand that *you*, under the direction of your spiritual guide, may use the violet light in a daily ritual of transmutation, thus removing all negativity and fear from your life.

Hold your crystal in your left hand and call to the violet light and ask that your spiritual guide focus the energy through your crystal and permit the power to connect you to your higher self.

Visualize the violet light moving over you in a wave of warmth. See it touching every part of your body. Feel it interacting with every cell.

Know that you may then say inwardly or aloud to your spiritual guide:

"Beloved guide, assist me in calling upon the highest of energies in the Source of All-That-Is. Activate my highest self to channel directly to Oneness. Stimulate the law of positive action for myself and all of us who stray from the light. Permit the violet light to move around and through me. Allow the transmutating energy to purify and to elevate all impure desires, incorrect concepts, anger, wrong-doing, improper memories and fears. Keep this light bright within me. Replace all negative, chaotic, fearful vibrations around me and in me with pure energy, the power of accomplishment, and the fulfillment of the Divine Plan."

Know that you may also utter this affirmation each morning upon arising:

"Beloved spiritual guide, I feel you on this new day, activating my higher self and charging me with perfect health, joy, love, the elimination of all fears, and the fulfillment of those physical things which I truly do need for my good and my gaining."

If you should feel discord coming upon you in a crowded place or in an environment wherein it is not immediately practical or possible to employ the Divine Flame of Transmutation in an effective manner, do the following:

Hold your crystal in your left hand and cross your arms over your solar plexus.

Put your knees or your feet together. (If you are sitting, cross your legs.)

The above actions instantly symbolize that you are not receptive to discord.

If you are in a social situation and you feel that a person present is seeking to bombard you with negativity and discord, 1. *hold* your crystal in your left hand,

2. *move* your arms across your solar plexus, 3. *cross* your knees if seated, 4. *visualize* a cross of blue flame dropping down from the heavens between you and the person or the condition that is afflicting you with negative vibrations.

Such immediate action can block the vicious energy that is being directed at you. In addition, take short breaths for a time, inhaling shallowly, but exhaling in a somewhat forceful manner. This procedure should not be practiced over-long, but with ample time to express your sentiments that you are not even breathing in the negativity that is being broadcast in your direction.

Let us say that you have been bombarded with negativity by a vicious person or by a situation that has left you feeling rather defeated and very much alone in the world. Perhaps you are away from home, and you feel that everyone in that strange environment is against you.

Go to your room or to a place where you can re-establish your emotional and spiritual equilibrium. Sit quietly for a moment. If possible, play some soft, restful music. It is always good to travel with your cassette player and a number of New Age music albums in your suitcase.

After you have begun to calm yourself, take your crystal in your lefthand and inhale, "I am." On the outbreath, say "relaxed."

Repeat this procedure a number of times. Take comfortably deep breaths. *"I am,"* asserting your sovereignty and your individual reality on the intake: *"relaxed"* positively affirming your calm condition on the outtake.

Now gaze into your crystal and visualize someone who is extremely positive and who shares your philosophy, your perspective, your point of view about life and the cosmos. This may be a spouse, a friend, a business associate, a teacher.

See the person on whom you are focusing turning toward you with a smile of love. See the person extending his or her hand to yours.

Feel the touch of fingertip to fingertip. Sense the electrical crackle of energy moving between you. Experience the warmth of the love that flows from entity to entity.

Visualize your taking that person's hand in your own. Feel comfortable knowing that there is one who loves you and who exhibits concern for you.

See this shared love erecting a barrier between you and the negative bombardment to which you have been subjected that day.

Columba Krebs

Crystals can be used to focus the Divine Fire and bring out illumination and the elimination of any negativity.

Next image you or your friend reaching forth a hand to take another's. Visualize yet another like-minded man or woman who is being welcomed to your circle. See that person joining you, smiling as he or she takes a place beside you to add to your fortress of bonded energy.

Continue to image other men and women joining your circle until you have built as large a barrier as you feel that you need to face the hostility or the negativity that is being directed against you in this strange and unfamiliar environment. Feel strength, born of love, swell within your breast.

Visualize energy moving from member to member of your magic circle. See the Golden Light of Protection encircling your group externally. See the energy of unconditional love flowing from one to another as you image yourself holding hands and linking your vibratory frequency to that of others of your spiritual philosophy.

After you have seen and felt the energy moving among your circle, visualize the ultraviolet light of the Source of All-That-Is descending from above and touching each of your members on the Crown Chakra.

Feel yourself vibrating with the greatest emanation of love from the very heart of the Universe.

Hold this image and this energy as long as is needed.

When you have become completely fortified and calmed, it would be best to go to bed and enjoy a peaceful night's rest.

If this is impossible and you must return to the encounter, know that you will do so totally prepared and reinforced for any situation which might arise. Stride confidently into the "arena," knowing that you are linked together in an unbreakable bond of love with those kindred souls who share your perspective and your goals.

EXPLORE THE FUTURE WITH CRYSTAL VISION

Using a larger crystal. breathe your intention to envision the future into its multifaceted form. Place the crystal before a candle and cradle it in both hands. Repeat the breathing process three times.

Begin to gaze within the crystal with your intention of gaining a glimpse of the World of Tomorrow. Sense the presence of your spiritual guide beginning to manifest around you.

Now take a smaller crystal in your left hand and lightly touch the larger one on the projecting tip. Breathe your intention of viewing the future into the smaller crystal and perceive the energy of the two blending and interacting with one another. Perceive their combined energy field expanding the electromagnetic field which surrounds your own physical body. Visualize your aura becoming a bright bluish color.

Place your right hand upon the larger crystal. Lightly touch the smaller crystal which you hold in your lefthand to your "third eye" area in the center of your forehead. Mentally ask your spiritual guide to lead your essential self, your soul, into the future.

Begin to relax the body as a friend reads the following visualization aloud. Once again, if you prefer, you may record your own voice reading this process into a tape recorder so that it is your own vibration that will guide you through the relaxation and projection process. Ethereal, futuristic music will be a great asset. Just be certain that your background music has no lyrics to distract you.

Permit yourself to relax completely. Use the technique previously provided in this chapter or any other method that totally relaxes you.

The Real You within your physical structure is becoming aware of a beautiful figure robed in violet standing near your relaxed body.

This beautiful figure is surrounded by an aura, a halo of golden light, and you know at once that you are beholding a guide who has come to take the *Real You* out of your physical shell and to travel with you to a higher dimension where you will be able to receive knowledge of a future life that you need to know about.

This may be a future life in which you may see a good many men and women who are with you in your present life. You may, in that future time, be completing a task left unfinished, learning a lesson left unaccomplished in your present life experience.

Whatever you see, it will be for your good and your gaining; and your guide will be ever near, allowing nothing to harm you. Your guide will be ever ready to protect you.

Now you permit your guide to take you by your hand and to lift the *Real You* out of your body.

Don't worry. Your spirit--the *Real You*--will always return to your body, but for now you are free to soar into the future, totally liberated of time and space.

The swirling purple mist is moving all around you;

and hand in hand with your guide, you begin to move higher and higher, higher and higher.

You seem to be floating through space, moving gently through space, moving through all of time.

Time itself seems to be like a spiral moving around you, a spiral never ending, never beginning, never ending, never beginning.

You know that you have the ability to move forward through time and to see a future life that you need to know about for your good and your gaining. A future life that may tell you very much about your present life.

Ahead of you, suspended in space, is a great golden door. And you know that when you step through that door you will be able to explore an important future life time.

You will be able to see the reasons why your soul will choose the parents, the brothers and sisters, the friends, the mate, the nationality, the race, the sex, the talents, the occupation of that future time.

You will see the soul-chosen purpose for the agonies, troubles, pains, and griefs that will enter that future life.

Now your guide is ushering you to the great golden door. The door is opening, and you step inside....

You see yourself as you will be when you are a child in that life.

If it is for your good and your gaining, you are able to know what country in which you will live--as you would understand it today--and what period of time it will be--as you would understand it today.

You see the color of your eyes, your hair, your skin. You see clearly what sex you are.

Now see your body unclothed. See if you have any scars, birthmarks, or other peculiar characteristics that are visible on your naked body.

Now you are clothed. See yourself in characteristic clothing for that future time. See clearly what is on your feet.

A man and a woman are now approaching you. Look at their eyes. It is the man and woman who are your *father and mother* in *that* life.

Understand what kind of relationship you have with them. Do they love you? Understand you? Reject you?

And now, for your good and your gaining look at their eyes and see if either of them are with you in your present-life experience and have rejoined you in that future time to complete work left unfinished...to master a lesson left unlearned.

Now, in that same future lifetime, scan the vibrations of any other relative and see if any other family member from that time is with you in your present life.

In that same future lifetime you are growing older, moving into young adulthood, and you see yourself performing some *favorite activity*, a game, a sport, a hobby, that becomes so very much a part of your life.

You see yourself performing that activity, and you understand how it will become impressed on your future life pattern.

You are now beginning to see clearly and to understand what *work* you will do in that life...how you will provide for yourself or for others...how you will spend your days.

Someone is approaching you from that work situation. Look into the eyes.

This may be someone who is your employer, your boss, your overseer.

This may be someone who is your employee.

But this is someone with whom you will interact closely at your work.

For your good and your gaining, look at the eyes; see if this person is with you in your present-life experience and has rejoined you to complete work left undone, to learn a lesson left unaccomplished.

As you move away from your work situation, you are beginning to feel the *vibrations of love* moving all around you. You are aware of someone standing there, to your left, standing there in the shadows.

You are feeling love--warm, peaceful sensations of love--moving all around you, as you realize that standing there in the shadows is the person whom you will love most in that lifetime.

Look at the eyes. Feel the love flowing toward you from those beautiful eyes of your beloved.

Look at the smile of recognition on those lips as the beloved one sees you and begins to move toward you.

This is the one with whom you will share your most intimate moments--your hopes, your dreams, your moments of deepest love. And yes, your sorrows, your hurts, your moments of deepest pain.

This is the one who will always care, who will always love and support you.

Go to these arms. Feel those beloved arms around you. Feel those lips on yours.

Now, for your good and your gaining, look at the eyes. See if this beloved one is with you in your present-life experience.

See if your love, like a golden cord, will stretch across time, space, generations, years, to reunite you in the same beautiful love vibrations.

See if you have come together again to work out a task left incomplete, a lesson left unlearned.

With a flash of insight your guide is showing you *why* you will live that life and why you will live it with those with whom you do.

You see clearly *why* you had to come again to put on the fleshly clothes of Earth in a future life.

You see *why* certain people from that life are with you now, and why they will rejoin you to complete work left undone, to master a lesson left unlearned.

In another flash of insight you are seeing and understanding *why* you came to Earth for the very *first* time, centuries ago.

You are remembering *why* you chose to put on the Karmic vibrations of Earth and come to this planet for the very first time.

You are remembering clearly *why* you came here. You are remembering your true mission in life.

You see and understand clearly what you are to do in your present life that will most aid you to accomplish your mission.

You are filled with a wonderful sense of well-being for now you know what you must do. You see clearly what you *must* do to fulfill totally your true mission in life. You no longer feel sensations of frustration and anxiety.

Now you *know*. You know why you came to Earth, why you chose to put on the clothes of Earth, why you chose to assume the Karmic vibration of this planet.

You are beginning to awaken, feeling very, very good.. very, very positive.

You are filled with a beautiful, glowing sense of your mission.

You are filled with the positive knowledge that you will be able to accomplish so much more good and gaining toward your true mission now that you are filled with awareness of your future lifetime.

Now you understand so very much more of the great pattern of your total life experience.

And you know that your guide will aid you, will assist you in completing your life mission, in accomplishing what you truly came here to do.

Awaken with positive feelings of love, wisdom, and knowledge. *Awaken* feeling very, very good in the body, mind, and spirit. *Awaken* feeling better than you have felt in weeks, in months, in years. *Awaken* filled with love, filled with knowledge.

THE CRYSTAL CAPSTONE ON THE PYRAMID OF LOVE

This process becomes a kind of universal blessing of unconditional love which you are able to transmit to the world.

Hold your crystal in your left hand and focus your attention upon its tip, the miniature pyramid that exists in each crystal. Imagine that it is actually the crystal capstone that once existed upon the Great Pyramid of Giza. See representatives of an ancient, but advanced technology, place the capstone into position. You might even perceive extraterrestrials setting the great crystal atop the massive pyramid.

As you gaze at the tip of your crystal, you are feeling very pleasant waves of warmth moving throughout your body.

Now visualize a beautiful golden pyramid manifesting directly above your head, immediately above your Crown Chakra. Understand that this pyramid is filled with Love from the Source of All-That-Is. Feel this great love from the very center of the Cosmos beaming down into your Crown Chakra.

And now sense the warmth of the universal love moving down from your Crown Chakra into your chest, your Heart Chakra, and feel that love blending with your own and streaming out of your heart Chakra to touch the heart of another. Know that you have made a positive love connection with another. Focus upon another person near you and know that you have touched that person with love.

Understand clearly that the more love you issue forth from your Heart Chakra, the more love will stream down into your Crown Chakra from the Golden Pyramid of Love with its Crystal Capstone of pure love energy from the Source. The more love you transmit, the more love will be poured into you from the Golden Pyramid directly above your Crown Chakra.

And now visualize a dear one who needs healing. Picture your love like a golden cord unwinding from your Heart Chakra and making positive connection with this loved one who needs the healing energy. See this person responding to your love connection.

Visualize someone who is lonely, fearful of life. Touch that person with your love. Let that person know that somewhere there is one who cares, who transmits love.

See your love traveling around the world, touching those who need love, connecting with those who need to feel that they are not alone.

And once the great circle has been completed, see that your love has orbited back to the Golden Pyramid above your Crown Chakra, once again filling you with love from the Source of All-That-Is, from the very center of the universe.

FOCUSING THE DIVINE FIRE

Yes, it is even possible to receive illumination from your practice of High Magick through crystals.

Take a crystal in each hand and gently place them against your temples. Close your eyes and take three comfortably deep breaths.

Lower the crystals and hold them a few inches away from your Heart Chakra. Now breathe your intention to achieve an illumination experience into the crystals. Repeat the process three times.

Set the crystals before you. See that their tips are lightly touching. Light a candle and place it three inches directly in front of the point where the two crystals almost meet.

Take three comfortably deep breaths and lower your head toward the larger of the crystals. *Image yourself being drawn into the larger crystal.* Visualize that your own energy is blending with the electromagnetic impulses of the crystal and that you are being pulled into the crystal.

Visualize yourself becoming one with the crystal energy for at least three minutes before you have a friend read the following process aloud to you. As before, you may record your own voice to serve as your guide. It is also suggested that some appropriate New Age inspirational music provide background score to heighten the effect.

Permit yourself to relax...totally and completely.

You will now invite the DIVINE FIRE to enter your psyche and enable you to become your own guru, your own instrument of balance, love, peace, strength, and inspiration.

You know that you have within you the ability to receive a spark of the DIVINE FIRE.

You know that you have the ability to be elevated to higher realms of consciousness and spiritual communion.

You know that you have the ability to become one with THE SOURCE OF ALL THAT IS.

You know that you have the ability to tap into the eternal transmission of Universal Truths from which you may draw power and strength.

You know that you have the ability to evolve as a spiritual being.

You know that you have the ability to progress out of your old, physical limitations and to rise to a higher realm.

Visualize yourself now as the kind of spiritual seeker with whom you most identify. You have this ability.

You have the ability to see yourself as a MONK of the European, Mid-Eastern, Indian, or Oriental traditions.

You have the ability to see yourself as a NUN, PRIESTESS, ORACLE, or COSMIC CHANNEL.

You have the ability to see yourself as a disciplined traditional AMERICAN INDIAN on a Vision Quest.

You have the ability to see yourself as a DRUID, a WICCAN, a practitioner of True Magick.

Perhaps you may wish to see yourself as an enlightened ALCHEMIST, traveling through Time and Space. Whatever the image you prefer, visualize yourself as that kind of SPIRITUAL SEEKER.

Slowly, you become aware of a presence. Someone has approached you and has come to stand next to you. Wherever you see yourself now...a forest clearing, a humble cell in a monastery or convent, a temple garden, a high mountain plateau--you are aware that *someone* stands near you as you rest.

As you look up at the figure, you see that it is a most impressive individual. It is a man who is looking at you with warmth and compassionate interest. And now you notice that he has been joined by a woman who is equally impressive, almost majestic in appearance. She smiles at you, and you feel somehow as if she stands before you enveloped in the mother vibration.

Before you can open your mouth to speak, the man and the woman fade from your sight. They simply disappear.

And now you realize that they were spirits, that they came to you from the spirit world to demonstrate to you that, in many ways, on many levels, you have a subtle, yet intense, partnership with the world of spirits. The spirit man and spirit woman have given you a visual sign of the reality of this Oneness with all *spiritual* forms of life.

You have but a moment to ponder the significance of the spirit visitation when you become aware of two globes of bluish-white light moving toward you. You are not afraid, for you sense a great spiritual presence approaching you.

As you watch in reverential expectation, the first globe of bluish-white light begins to assume a human form. As the light swirls and becomes solid, you behold before you a man or a woman whom you regard as a Holy Person, a saint, a master, an illumined One.

This figure, so beloved to you, gestures to your left side. As you turn, you are astonished to see a marvelous linkup of other Holy Figures, from all times, from all places, from all cultures. You see that these personages form a beautiful spiritual chain, from prehistory to the present, and, without doubt, the future.

The Holy One smiles benevolently, then bends over you and touches your shoulder. Then, gently, the Holy One's forefinger lightly touches your eyes, then your ears, then your mouth. You know that this touching symbolizes that you are about to see and to hear a wondrous revelation, which, consequently, you must share with others.

As the Holy Figure begins to fade from your perception, the second globe of bluish-white light begins to materialize into human form.

The entity that forms before you now may be very familiar to you. You may very likely have seen this entity in your dreams. You may even have seen this entity materialize before you on previous occasions.

You may have been aware of this entity since your earliest memories, for standing before you now is your guide.

See the love in those eyes. *Feel* the love emanating toward *you* from your guide. This is one who has *always* loved you--just as you are. This is one who has always totally accepted you--just as you are. This is one, who, with unconditional love, is concerned completely with your spiritual evolution. You feel totally relaxed, at peace, at One with your guide. And you feel totally loved.

Your guide's mouth is opening. *Listen.* Listen to the sound that issues forth. You hear it clearly and you understand it. It may be a personal sound--a mantra. It may be a series of notes and words--your own personal song of attunement. It may be your guide's name.

Whatever the sound is, you hear it clearly and distinctly. And you have the inner awareness that whenever you repeat this sound--this mantra, this song, this name--you will be able to achieve instant At-Oneness with your guide.

Your guide is now showing you something important. Your guide's hands are holding something for you to see. It is an object which you can clearly identify which will serve as a symbol to you in your dreams. It will serve as a symbol that you are about to receive a meaningful and important teaching in your dreams. Whenever you see this symbol in your dreams, you will understand that an important and significant teaching will follow.

That symbol fades from your sight, but you *will* remember it.

You are fascinated by what your guide now holds before you. In your guide's hands is a tiny flame, a flame such as one might see on a match or a candle. The flame flickers and dances. You cannot take your eyes from it. The flame seems to capture all of your attention and to pull you toward it. It is as if your very spirit is being pulled from your body and drawn toward the flame.

The flame is becoming brighter--brighter and larger. You cannot take your eyes from this strange, compelling flame. You can no longer see your guide. You can see only the flame. You are no longer aware of anything other than the flame. It is growing larger, larger and brighter, brighter and larger. It is as if there is nothing else in the entire universe but the flame--the flame and *you*.

You know now that this is the Divine Fire. You know now that this flame has appeared to bring you illumination. You know that it is not really a fire, not really a flame. but a divine and holy energy, the same energy that is interwoven with all of life, the same energy that interacts with all of life. This energy now swirls around you, lightly tingling the body whenever it touches you. It is not at all an unpleasant sensation. It is, in fact, soothing yet strangely exhilerating at the same time.

The energy now caresses your body, gently, lovingly. You are aware of your body becoming cleansed, purified, healed of any ills, pains, and tensions. You know that from this moment onward, your physical health is going to be superb, better than it has ever been. You know that from this moment on, your physical energy is going to be increased. You know that your friends and your family will be commenting about your golden glow of health and vitality.

The energy of the Divine Fire now enters your body. It is now becoming One with you. It is becoming one with your cleansed and purified body. It is becoming one with your expectant spirit.

In a great rush of color and light, you now find yourself elevated in spirit. You have moved to a dimension where non-linear time, cyclical time, flows around you. From your previous limited perspective of Earth-time, linear time, you are aware that you now exist in a Timeless Realm, an Eternal Now.

At this eternal second in the energy of the Eternal Now, at this vibrational level of Oneness with all living things, at this frequency of awareness of unity with the Cosmos, the Divine Fire is permitting *you* to receive a great teaching vision of something about which you need to know for your good and your gaining. Receive this great vision--*now!*

You will awaken at the count of five, filled with memories of your great vision. When you awaken you will feel morally elevated; you will feel intellectually illuminated; you will know that your essence is immortal; you will no longer fear death; you will no longer experience guilt or a sense of sin; you will feel filled with a great charm and personal magnetism; you will feel better and healthier than ever before in your life; you will feel a great sense of unity with *all* living things.

One...two...three...four...five...awaken!

TRAVEL TO OUTER SPACE IN YOUR OWN CRYSTAL STARSHIP

Be certain that the only illumination in the room is a single candle that you have placed directly before your crystal. Some New Age music suggestive of space travel or outer space itself would be extremely effective in achieving the full benefit of this process.

Take your crystal in your left hand and breathe your intention of traveling to outer space into its electromagnetic essence. Repeat this process three times as you rotate the crystal.

Lift the crystal to eye-level and project your intention mentally as well. Imagine that you can see an entire cosmos within your crystal. See spiraling nebulae, galaxies, constellations, thousands of sparkling stars--all there within your crystal. Imagine that in your left hand you hold a tiny, but complete, universe.

Now take three comfortably deep breaths and commence a relaxation process. **Permit yourself to relax totally, completely, before you allow a friend or your own prerecorded** voice to lead you through your odyssey through outer space.

You are gazing upward at the night sky. You begin to notice a particularly brilliant, flashing star high overhead. As you watch it, it seems to be moving toward you. It seems to be lowering itself to you.

Now you see that it is not a star at all. It is a large, beautifully glowing crystal starship. You feel no fear, only expectation. You feel secure in the love of the Universe. You feel unconditional love, as the object with the sparkling, swirling lights lowers itself near you. You know that it is a vehicle that has come to take you to levels of higher awareness.

A door is opening in the side of the Crystal Light Vehicle. You look inside and see that it is lined with plush, soft velvet. You know that it is safe. You know that it is comfortable. And it glows within with the golden light of protection, the light of unconditional love from the very heart of the Universe.

Step inside, settle back against the soft, comfortable cushions. The door silently closes, and you know that the vehicle will now begin to take you to those higher levels of consciousness. You are completely comfortable, relaxed, soothed, but you know that you are being taken higher and higher, higher to total awareness.

You look out of a small window at your side, and you see Earth below you becoming smaller and smaller, as you rise higher and higher. Colors seem to be moving around you. Stars seem to be moving around you.

You feel love, pure, unconditional love all around you. You are being taken to a dimension of higher consciousness. You are being taken to a vibration of a finer, more highly realized, awareness. You know that you are safe. You know that some Benevolent Force is taking you to the Timeless Realm where visions live. You know that you will be safely returned to Earth once you have been to the In-Between Universe, the In-Between Dimension where teaching-visions await you. Colors swirl around you. Stars swirl around you. You are moving across the galaxy.

You are traveling higher and higher, higher into the very Soul of the Universe. You know that you will receive meaningful Teaching Visions when you reach that Timeless Realm where visions live.

Before beginning your trip to Outer Space in your own
Crystal Starship, visualize a cosmos within your crystal.

And now your Light Vehicle has come to a stop. You look out your window and see that you have stopped before a beautiful golden door, a door that seems to be suspended in Space.

You know that when you step through the beautiful golden door, you will find yourself in the Timeless Realm where Visions await you. You know that you will have the ability to perceive and to comprehend meaningful teaching-visions, visions designed especially to provide you with deep and profound insights and understandings.

When you step through the golden door, you will enter a dimension which exists on a higher vibration...and your mind will be totally attuned to that frequency. You will have the ability to receive clear and revelatory visions. You will receive the answers to questions which you have asked for so very, very long.

When you step through that golden door, you will enter a realm where magnificent, colorful panoramas of living diagrams and teachings of awareness will be given to you. Unconditional love will permeate your entire being. Angels, guides, master-teachers will interact with you, share with you, teach you.

And now the golden door is beginning to open. A panel in your Light Vehicle is sliding back, permitting you to leave its interior, allowing you to step through the golden door.

You know that you are protected, you know that you are guided, you know that you are loved. You step from your Light Vehicle, and you step inside the Golden Door.

As you step inside, you know that you have the ability to perceive and to understand profound teaching-visions.

As you step inside, the first sight that awaits you is the view of a marvelous *crystal transformer*, a crystal tube that is a very special vehicle which will take you even deeper into this Timeless Realm. This crystal transformer will take you into the place of ultimate awareness where the Teaching Visions await you.

You know that when you enter this crystal tube and move higher into the Timeless Realm, some teachings may be given to you in words, *without* an accompanying vision. These will be insights, thought-forms of encapsuled awareness. Other teachings may be given to you in visual thought-forms, living diagrams.

Stand before the crystal tube.

Stand before this very special transforming vehicle that will take you to the exact place where visions live, where only love exists, where you will have the ability to receive your vision teachings.

A panel in the side of the crystal tube, the crystal transformer, is sliding back to permit you to enter. You know that you will be guided and protected. You know that you will be safe. You know that you want to receive the answers to so many questions, answers which your vision-teachings will provide.

Step inside the crystal tube and feel unconditional love all around you. Lie back against the soft lining of the tube. Make yourself totally comfortable. The panel slides softly, silently closed, and you begin to move to the special place where visions live.

You are moving *out*...you are moving *out* now...or is it really IN?

Stars seem to sparkle around you. Stars seem to move around you.

And now it seems as though the Crystal Transformer, the crystal tube has disappeared, and you are hanging suspended in space...totally protected by the golden light of unconditional love from the very heart of the Universe. And you have the ability to receive your first teaching vision.

The FIRST LIVING DIAGRAM appears, sent to you by the SOURCE OF ALL THAT IS...This living diagram explains to you THE TRUE NATURE OF THE SOUL...THE TRUE NATURE OF THE SOUL AND WHAT REALLY HAPPENS TO THE SPIRIT AFTER THE PHYSICAL DEATH OF THE BODY.

You are seeing now your true relationship to your Soul...your Soul's relationship to your guides...to God...to the Universe. You are seeing yourself making the physical transition of death in a PAST life, and you see and understand what truly happens to the spirit at the moment of physical death.

Now your SECOND TEACHING VISION is beginning to manifest. The second living diagram explains to you, THE TRUE NATURE OF OTHER INTELLIGENCES IN THE UNIVERSE.

You may see alien lifeforms. You may be focusing in on a planet, a city, a people, a culture...all of which are alien to Earth. You are seeing an alien people-...you are seeing their history, their customs, their belief structures, their methods of transportation.

Your THIRD TEACHING-VISION appears, your third living diagram begins to form. This third vision explains to you, YOUR MOST IMPORTANT PAST LIFE, YOUR KARMIC COUNTERPART.

This is the past life experience which has been the most influential on your present life experience. This is the Sower for whom you have been reaping. You will be shown, and you will understand, the importance of this previous life experience in terms of your Soul's evolution to the SOURCE OF ALL THAT IS. You will see details that will help you to understand your present life experience. You will see details that will help you to see why you are the way you are...why things have progressed the way they have progressed. You will see WHO came with you and WHY.

Your FOURTH LIVING, TEACHING-VISION is showing you scenes from FUTURE TIME. You are being shown THE FACE OF THE EARTH IN THE NEW AGE.

You are seeing this planet as it will look after the Earth Changes have fully taken place. You are being shown changes in society...art...politics...economics... clothing styles. You are being shown the skyline of cities. You will not be shocked by anything that you may see...even if cities are underground...even if new coastlines have been formed...even if new mountain ranges have appeared...even if new people walk among us. You will see and you will understand.

From the vantage point of looking backward from the Future, you will now see where the safe places will be. Look at a map of the United States...Canada...wherever you wish. The SAFE PLACES will glow with a golden energy. See and understand where the safe places will be.

And as you gaze into the FUTURE, you have the ability now to see an important FUTURE LIFE EXPRESSION OF YOUR SOUL. You are being shown an important future life experience that your soul will live on Earth...or elsewhere.

You have the ability to see yourself and to know what you are wearing...the color of your hair and eyes...whether you are male or female--or androgynous. You see your environment. Your domestic life-support systems. And you see WHO is with you from your present life experience or from any previous life experience.

And now your FIFTH LIVING DIAGRAM appears. You will now receive insights as to YOUR TRUE MISSION ON EARTH...WHY YOU REALLY CAME TO THIS PLANET IN THE FIRST PLACE.

You will be shown, and you will understand, why and when you first chose to put on the fleshly clothes of Earth. You will see why and when your first chose to enter the Karmic Laws which bind this planet. You will see and you will understand what it is that you are to accomplish in your Soul's evolution in this place of learning.

And now your CRYSTAL TRANSFORMER has reappeared. Once again it appears to be solid around you. It has come to take you back to Earth Time, back to Human Time, back to Present Time, back to your present life experience.

You will remember all that you need to know for your good and your gaining.

You will be strengthened to face the challenges and the learning experiences of your life.

And know this: *The more you share your visions and your teachings, the more your understanding of them will grow.*

You are now awakening, surrounded by Light and by Love, by pure, unconditional Love. You feel very, very good in mind, body, and spirit. You feel better than you have felt in weeks, months and months, years and years.

You will awaken fully at the count of FIVE.

Brad establishes a focal point with his own individual healing crystal.

In the great days of ancient Egypt it is believed that giant crystals were placed at the top of the pyramids and were utilized as energy devices and as beacons for star travelers. (Art by Carol Ann Rodriguez)